THE HOBBIT ™

THE BATTLE OF THE FIVE ARMIES

Other publications from Weta include:

The Hobbit: An Unexpected Journey:
Chronicles: Art & Design

The Hobbit: An Unexpected Journey:
Chronicles: Creatures & Characters

The Hobbit: The Desolation of Smaug:
Chronicles: Art & Design

The Hobbit: The Desolation of Smaug:
Chronicle Companion:
Smaug, Unleashing the Dragon

The Hobbit: The Desolation of Smaug:
Chronicles: Cloaks & Daggers

Coming 2015:
The Hobbit: The Battle of the Five Armies:
Chronicle VI

HarperCollins*Publishers*
77–85 Fulham Palace Road,
Hammersmith, London W6 8JB
www.tolkien.co.uk

Published by HarperCollins*Publishers* 2014
1

THE HOBBIT

THE BATTLE OF THE FIVE ARMIES

CHRONICLES ❖ ART & DESIGN

INTRODUCTION BY JOHN HOWE

FOREWORD BY BOB BUCK   WRITTEN BY DANIEL FALCONER

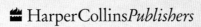 HarperCollins*Publishers*    WETA
www.wetaNZ.com

CONTENTS

Acknowledgements

Five *Chronicles*! It seems like only last month our little team began on this journey to tell the stories behind the story of *The Hobbit*. I can say with complete honesty that it has been a pleasure putting together such beautiful books filled with such beautiful imagery, and it is all because I have the pleasure of working with such a beautiful team. Sincerest thanks to my collaborators in this endeavour, the incomparably good-humoured Monique Hamon, Fiona Ogilvie and Kate Jorgensen. With a tear in the eye we say farewell to Kate as this is wrapped up, thanking her for making this all possible and keeping the Weta Publishing boat steered true these past four years. At the same time we welcome Karen Flett to our team, who has already made herself invaluable in the choreographing of this newest title in the series.

I wish to express my appreciation for the continued friendship and sage assistance of our UK HarperCollins*Publishers* team on the other side of the world: Chris Smith, David Brawn, Terence Caven, Kathy Turtle and Stuart Bache, as well as Marta Schooler in the USA.

Thanks to our amazing supporters at home within Weta Workshop, Richard Taylor, Tim Launder, Tasha Guillot, Rik Athorne, and Weta Digital's Penelope Scott. Thank you also to the patient and diligent folks at 3Foot7, Wingnut Films and Warner Bros., upon whom we rely so heavily in pulling together and approving the content of these books: Matt Dravitzki, Amanda Walker, Judy Alley, Melissa Booth, Anna Houghton, Susannah Scott, Jill Benscoter, Elaine Piechowski, Victoria Selover and Melanie Swartz.

Of course, there would be no *Hobbit: Chronicles* if there were no *Hobbit* movies. Sincerest thanks to Peter Jackson, Fran Walsh and Philippa Boyens for creating a film trilogy's worth of awesomeness for us to imagine, make and write about.

Finally, sincerest appreciation to the amazing artists whose work fills every page of this book with wonder. It has been an honour to spend time with you all and talk with you about your craft and ideas. I truly appreciate the time you have given me in the midst of busy schedules, and in particular thank Alan Lee and John Howe, who so politely and good-naturedly suffered my continual harassment! I hope every artist whose work is included here can be proud of the way their art and ideas are represented. Thanks for trusting me to tell your stories.

Daniel Falconer

FOREWORD

BB
CD

Welcome to the fifth behind-the-scenes Chronicle of *The Hobbit* film trilogy. Within these pages you will be taken on a detailed journey through Middle-earth along the creative paths travelled by a fellowship of many who collaborated to bring you the final instalment in *The Hobbit* film trilogy.

For me *The Battle of the Five Armies* marks the end of a personal journey that began more than sixteen years earlier, when I first became involved in the world of Tolkien.

Working at both Weta Workshop and the Costume Department on *The Lord of the Rings*, one of my primary tasks was to bring the Dwarven race to life. Many talented technicians, sculptors, pattern cutters and textile artists pooled their considerable skills, experimenting, sampling and inventing fabrics, developing chainmaille and playing with proportions to establish the design ethos and aesthetic of this noble, earthy, but displaced race. However, in *The Lord of the Rings* there was only one hero Dwarf character, Gimli, and a handful of featured Dwarf extras, so, as far as establishing the Dwarves as a fully developed culture, there was only so much that we could showcase.

For me, and so many of the team members who worked on the first trilogy, *The Hobbit*, and especially *The Battle of the Five Armies*, was a wonderful opportunity to revisit those original ideas about the Dwarves and develop them further, digging deeper into the richness and gravitas of the kingdom of Erebor. The Dwarves of the Company of Thorin have now

reached their former homeland and returned to the Great Halls of their ancestors, and we could now fully celebrate the wealth and extreme craftsmanship of the culture, culminating in the battle itself. Here they would take on the garments of their forebears, accepting the mantle of their heritage, and fight to protect both that which they have reclaimed and their very lives.

There is a definite sense of coming full circle for me with this final film as well as a huge sense of pride and privilege to have been able to be involved creatively in both film trilogies and have shared the experience and challenges with such an impressive group of talented people. This book celebrates our collaboration and highlights the fact that the creative process is not a linear one. The designs that were never realized are as important as the ones that were, being part of the process and representing the elimination or germination of an idea that grew into the visuals as seen on the screen. Within these pages you will find a rich and deep gallery of imagery and stories that express the creativity, coordination, hard work, research, intuition and luck of a large design community.

Enjoy!

**Bob Buck,
Costume Designer**

INTRODUCTION
BEYOND WILDERLAND

Even the longest journeys, it seems, start with a single sketch. Five years ago, Alan Lee and I began putting pencils to paper, letting them wander over the white page until scenes appeared, not unlike a lifting of fog, when the sun suddenly lends clarity to both thoughts and vistas. Five years on, we are not *quite* back again; where on earth *have* we been in the meantime?

We started in familiar country: round doors and windows, a pleasant inn, the familiar sight of Bag End, though last time we had not visited the cellar or the dining room, or discovered five new hobbit dwellings further down the lane from Bilbo's house.

We made a detour through deep Greenwood to see ramshackle Rhosgobel, belonging to the ragtag *Istar* Radagast, a house split in half by an awkwardly placed sapling become venerable forest giant: askew, propped up and slowly returning to the wildwood.

Then on (with an interlude with a trio of Trolls, and with Orcs & Wargs in pursuit) to take refuge in another familiar spot: Rivendell, though we drew much that we had not seen that other time through. Then from there, the first steps into territories unknown, towards the Misty Mountains, taking shelter from Stone Giants in a slightly-too-handy cavern. A moment's pause, then a tumble, a capture, a confrontation and a rescue, followed by a madcap dash along teetering bridges over unsavoury depths – hastily sketching ricketty walkways, impossible precipices, the whole in a sidewise cavern eroded through the mountains, followed by the collapse of the final bridge and ending in a jumble of rubble at the chasm bottom. All this drawn, or at least it felt like it, at a breakneck pace. Then out of the frying pan, and of course, Wargs hot on our heels (again), fire in the pine trees and… saved. Eagles. Pencils stilled, we contemplated the mountains and valleys of Middle-earth that floated underneath as the sun rose, before quickly drawing a Carrock on which to land.

From that outcrop, Mirkwood is still but a smudge on the horizon, but closer to hand, behind a thick thorny hedge, the house of the skin-changer Beorn, built of huge squared logs, every inch carved with knotwork and creatures, all reminiscent of the Nine Worlds and the Perilous Wood, a reminder we are at last truly in Wilderland. We draw the edge of Mirkwood, then the path inwards, the road is quickly lost in a twisted host of trunks hiding a Styx-like stream flowing with Lethe's black waters, before again the Dwarves are captured, first nabbed and trussed up and cruelly pinched by Spiders, then an instant after Bilbo saves their bacon, captured by Elves.

And away we go again in their wake, towards the Woodland Realm. We soon find out what it resembles: an elegant bridge and columns fashioned like trees, framing three bronze doors across a raging torrent. We have arrived in Thranduil's realm. We race across the bridge as the great doors swing to.

Inside, it looks like nothing we expected: the grand halls but cavern walls, no marble floors polished and wide, only great sinuous roots, it is like being in the nave of a cathedral, but in mid-air. Amber lamps pool the light. We get a glimpse of the throne, huge-antlered, enclosed in Gothic tracery, but are soon locked away deep underground, crammed into cubbyhole cells hollowed from a subterranean ravine and fitted with bronze bars. But escape is at hand; we draw keys for Bilbo to steal, bottles of deep wine poured into cups of amber and wood to inebriate the gaolers. Doors are unlocked; we steal off, first to cellars stacked with bottles and barrels, past our slumbering guardians, then to plunge into another wild rollercoaster escape, furiously drawing our way downriver through waterfalls, fortified gates and precipitous canals carved from cliff faces, until the calmer waters of the river are reached.

From there, a voyage by boat with a surly boatman, through looming and mysterious stone ruins on a fogbound lake, and the mist lifts again. Lake-town. It is a Renaissance Kiev built on a lake, a Venice all of wood, once prosperous, now a-kilter and sinking into the depths. It reminds us of stave churches, or the villages of the mythical Swiss lake dwellers, but with a hint of farther north and farther east. We are, after all, deep in Wilderland.

There is not much time to pause; we make directly for the Lonely Mountain, though all this time we have made detours: far south through Mirkwood, to Dol Guldur, the Hill of Sorcery. It is a horrid place, full of uncomfortable angles and unseemly proportions, littered with machines of torture and iron maidens suspended on rusty chain. We do not see the Necromancer, but everything we draw tells us who he really is. We follow Gandalf to the High Fells, in a hanging valley in Hithlaegir, the Misty Mountains, where kings were buried deep under hard stone, so as never to return from death. But the sarcophagi are broken and abandoned, the entombed have risen.

But there isn't time to waste, the ghostly ruins of Dale are a tragic and burnt shadow of the bright city we drew two years before. There is nothing here now, all burnt, all dust. We have drawn near to the Desolation of Smaug.

Erebor. The front door is shut by the fear of the lurking wyrm, but we drew a key to the back door, and the back door as well, hidden in plain sight behind a colossal statue of Thrór. We imagine other statues, like a Dwarven Valley of the Kings, but there is no time to draw them. The sun is almost down on Durin's day, we must hurry.

Then we are inside the Mountain, and down, down to the Dragon's lair. Erebor too is silent, and dark, and damp as a tomb, no trace of the splendid kingdom we drew years ago; now it is shadowed halls and carelessly broken statues.

Below, Smaug, Greatest of Calamities. He emerges little by little from the page. He is huge, and old, his eyes burn yellow, though his red-gold scales are dulled by time. We draw a veritable mountain of gold through which he slithers like some vast snake. We draw the great red-gold firedrake, thinking all the while of Fafnír and Beowulf's bane: acres of scales, vast webbed wings, teeth like swords and claws like iron. A dedicated and informal interdepartmental team builds, textures, rigs, animates and finally breathes life into Smaug the Terrible. (Yes, we will get Team Smaug t-shirts.)

Then Bilbo taunts the wyrm, and steals the cup. The battle is on, seemingly one-sided until the Dwarves light the great fires of Erebor's furnaces, and we find ourselves drawing a labyrinthine foundry Piranesi might have appreciated, with gushing waterspouts, hammers and bellows the size of houses, until Smaug, singed by a cascade of molten gold, bursts from the Mountain.

Bilbo let slip too many clues, Smaug is bound for Lake-town. And that's where we are: as I write this, I'm deep in Erebor and exploring the ruins of Dale, Alan is on the left-hand spur of the Lonely Mountain, plotting out Ravenhill. We are busily fortifying Erebor, preparing to burn Lake-town, the Black Arrow is drawn and ready; war is approaching. The Dwarves have just found the armoury, the Elves are coming, and the refugees of Lake-town are pouring into Dale. From Gundabad, a rust-red iron fortress shaped like a gigantic blade, an Orc army is streaming forth. We need to return as well to Dol Guldur, for unfinished business there...

We would eagerly go farther, to the Withered Heath where Dragon bones are strewn, or to the Iron Hills, to see Daín's stronghold, but the story is nearing an end.

Finally, when the adventure is over, and the mourners have left the Deep Tombs, we can stow away pencils and sketchbooks and retrace our steps to Bag End, to watch Bilbo wrest his silver spoons from Lobelia, and we'll be Back Again.

Naturally, we've never been alone in this adventure: in front of the camera and behind, an army of several thousand: designers and decorators, painters, carpenters and construction crews, sculptors in all media, fabricators, film crews, costumiers and craftspeople of all sorts, the seldom sung administrative wizards who keep the entire operation in motion, and the thousand-strong army whose considerable talents are brought to bear in post-production. Sketches become set designs, then sets, limned in green, decorated and lit, brief stops for the actors on their own journey. We have several chances to draw it all, often years apart; a portion of things imagined in pre-production, built of wood and poly and paint during production, then the rest of pixels in post. What we cannot see built for real, we can build in thin air, the real and the virtual end up so intertwined it's difficult to tell where one stops and the other starts.

And in a sense, they are the same; the ideas remain, only their realization differs. Looking back, it seems an impressive – or at least a lengthy – list of places imagined, but it is really only a minuscule part of the whole. We could never have imagined a land like New Zealand, so hauntingly familiar and so stunningly exotic. Nor re-invent or dream of bettering the thousands of years of human history, art and architecture upon which we built our flights of fancy. We could never imagine the people we would have the privilege to meet, creators and artists of all kinds from Weta Workshop, 3Foot7 and Weta Digital. Nor imagine the vital life brought to the sets by the actors (no, they don't have an easy job, and yes, they do possess something very special). Or do anything but envy the steadfast endurance and ever-fresh enthusiasm of the core production team, headed by Peter, Fran & Philippa. Nor of course can we imagine our own world without a book, written 77 years ago by an Oxford professor, and the millions upon millions of people who have made it a part of their imaginations.

All of those things, focused through a sharp pencil tip, wandering over a page, while the mind wanders through lands only imagined.

There. Back Again. It all begins with a sketch.

John Howe,
Concept Art Director

FIRE & WATER

THE BURNING OF LAKE-TOWN

'I am fire, I am … *Death*.'

Smaug the Terrible descends upon Lake-town in a storm of flame and wrath, obliterating wooden homes and workshops by the dozen with each pass. The devastation wrought by the Dragon in his fury is unlike anything imagined by the humble people of Esgaroth and they are plunged into chaos and terror.

There is but one weapon in the beleaguered town which could penetrate the monster's scaled hide, but the ancient wind lance of Dale is little more than a decoration atop the Master's great hall, lacking ammunition or a crew trained to use it, and Smaug is quick to destroy the artefact.

As their leader abandons Lake-town aboard his bulging treasure barge and the people throw themselves into the water to escape the conflagration there is just one man who has the courage and wisdom to mount a heroic defence. Imprisoned by the Master, Bard engineers an inventive escape and rushes across burning roofs to send his arrows at the Dragon.

Having designed and built Lake-town as a sprawling, ingeniously reconfigurable outdoor set, the 3Foot7 Art Department, under the supervision of Production Designer Dan Hennah, the on-set special effects crew and Weta Digital's artists were now faced with the challenge of destroying said construction in a manner that was repeatable and safe, while also appropriately epic in its catastrophic majesty. This would be a task achieved through a combination of work accomplished on the live back-lot set, on location on the shores of New Zealand's lake, and deep within the magical labyrinth of wonders that is Weta Digital.

In the wake of the devastation, an army of extras would be clothed and armed for war by the 3Foot7 Costume Department and Weta Workshop, the vengeance of the Dragon Smaug being but the first of the horrors to be visited upon them.

LAKE-TOWN

GAOL

Lake-town's jail was quite a small set but an interesting one because it wasn't only a cell. It was also a corridor and sat on a little bridge so that it hung over the water. The guardroom doubled as the armoury the Dwarves raided in the second film. When Bard makes his escape, he climbs along the front of the bridge and in through a guardroom window.

Alan Lee, Concept Art Director

Notes and documents in the Lake-town gaol (*below*) ranged from the business-like *Removal of Items* forms, delivery dockets and goods inventories to tallies of *rats caught in E-Block since midsummer*, lists of tasks to accomplish before the Master's next visit, some questionable mathematical calculations, and even some amateur poetry (hitherto unpublished).

Daniel Reeve, Graphic Artist

LAKE-TOWN BOATS & THE MASTER'S BARGE

Sometimes concept art needs to be produced very speedily. One of the Lake-town sets had been shot from every angle possible, yet needed to become a completely different area of the city for an 8:00a.m. start the next day.

4:30p.m.: explanation of what Peter wanted. 6:00p.m.: sketch finished, approved, scanned and given to the night crew supervisor.

Overnight, the set went from the square immediately in front of the Town Hall to a quay well across town, from where Thorin and his little Company make their triumphal departure, all ready for shooting the next day. Happily, we usually have much more time (and had I known I would spend three days in costume standing on it, I might have made the musician's platform a little wider).

Most of the boats in Lake-town were small, except for the Master's barge, and Bard's, which had to accommodate enough large barrels in which to smuggle thirteen Dwarves and one hobbit into Lake-town.

John Howe, Concept Art Director

Bard's barge was a very practical thing for picking up barrels and general work transporting goods around the town. It was a bulky-looking thing in contrast with the Master's barge.

There was an Eastern flavour to the little boats dotted around Lake-town. Many of the drawings we did were of little skiffs, low to the water and punted rather than rowed. I always liked the idea of them fishing with cormorants, so there were cormorants in almost all of my drawings as I did my best to get that idea across the line and have a model made by Weta Digital, but I had to make do with seagulls in the end.

Alan Lee, Concept Art Director

The Master's barge was more like a royal pleasure boat, the kind of thing in which you might see royalty being punted down a canal. We wanted to give it a feeling of pomp and ceremony. In the early days we had a cabin on it, at the rear, and quite a lot of design work was done on the interior of that. It also had a hold for the Master's hoarded treasures, but Peter very sensibly decided it was better to have the barge openly loaded down with stuff in a giant pile on the deck. It communicated what the Master was doing more obviously, so we piled the treasure on till the boat was almost sinking.

Indeed, the Master takes action to prevent this very thing when Alfrid informs him that they are too heavy and have to lose some weight. Considering Alfrid the most expendable item aboard, the Master promptly knocks him over the side!

Alan Lee, Concept Art Director

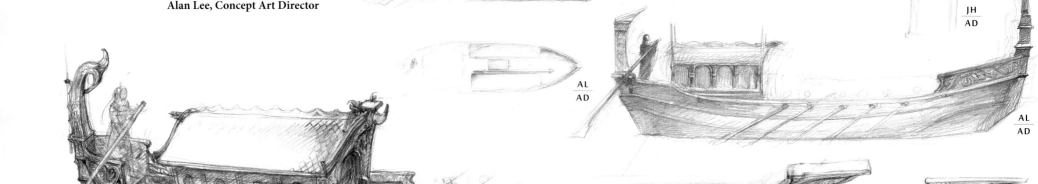

Throwing a homemade lasso, Bard ropes the stern of the barge and its inertia tears the bars from his prison cell, allowing him to escape. It was the Master who put him there so it is poetic that as the noose goes over the stern it also loops around Lake-town's fleeing leader as well.

Alan Lee, Concept Art Director

The Lake-town boats were mostly modest craft, with the exception of the Master's barge, which was the only boat in Esgaroth with a fresh coat of paint. It sported a fine figurehead of the Master himself, larger than life. Gilded friezes ran along the gunwales, and cherub supporters held his arms on the prow (the cherubs were modelled from baby pictures of one of the members of the Art Department).

John Howe, Concept Art Director

THE MASTER OF LAKE-TOWN

ARMOUR & WEAPONS

The Mayor of Lake-town never goes anywhere without protection of some sort. At one point there was supposed to be a scene where he would don armour. I imagined this armour would most likely have been made by the same craftsmen who worked on the armour for his bodyguards. I had fun dreaming up the most ostentatious and pompous armour possible, to fit his character.

Frank Victoria, Weta Workshop Designer

Frank Victoria and I were in a bit of a friendly competition to land the design of the Master of Lake-town's outrageous suit of armour. Although the idea was later scrapped, at the time the script called for the Master to have armour that he would wear to the battle. We saw it as an opportunity to design something over the top for Stephen Fry to wear. He was such a favourite with us: we all loved him. I was imagining a pompous and overblown version of King Henry VIII, with big fish shapes, tassels, plumes and gaudy colours.

Frank won and his design was built as a full suit, but the scene was dumped so tragically we never got to see Stephen strutting his stuff in it.

Paul Tobin, Weta Workshop Designer

THE MASTER'S BAND

We designed instruments for the Master's ramshackle little band of musicians. I imagined them as quite a motley crew of different shapes and sizes, united by a rough sort of uniform but holding an assemblage of odd instruments. Peter encouraged us to be wacky with them. We stuck with wind instruments as it was supposed to be a fanfare they were playing, so it became an assortment of trumpets and a serpent, which is a long, snake-like wooden thing.

The invitation for John Howe and me to actually join the band as extras came later. We joined David Donaldson and Steve Roche of Plan 9, a group who provided source music for the films. They handled their instruments like the professionals they were. I think I drew the short straw because I ended up with a sort of giant double trumpet (*below, right*) which was more an article of plumbing than a musical instrument. It weighed a ton and was rather top heavy. It was quite a job to hold that prop all day and pretend to blow it, but nonetheless, spending a day in costume beneath Stephen Fry doing his thing from his little podium was still a lot of fun.

Alan Lee, Concept Art Director

This was another fun brief to make the world of Middle-earth more interesting. What would the music of Lake-town sound like? It was highly enjoyable to create this set of musicians in costume. I also thought that this could be a good opportunity to include a woman musician, as *The Hobbit* doesn't describe many female characters.

Frank Victoria, Weta Workshop Designer

FV / WW

AL / AD

AL / AD   AL / AD

LAKE-TOWN

ROOFTOPS

The environments that in past films might have been realized through the use of miniatures were, in *The Hobbit*, all entirely digital, but nowhere did we come closer to using real miniatures than in Lake-town. The model-making team chose a few dozen buildings from the hundreds of sketches we did to create the various Lake-town concept models. The result was spectacular, with models that went far beyond the requirements of blocking out building structure and volumes, to become real miniatures summing up all of the spirit of Lake-town: once prosperous, now with rotting piles, sagging roofs and peeling paint, askew and sinking into the Long Lake. They took very much to heart the storytelling, and improved upon the original sketches with a true craftsman's touch, improvising repairs and additions, bringing real life to the structures themselves.

John Howe, Concept Art Director

The models were set out on vast tables, and their various arrangements constituted the base for the three large Lake-town sets. Fortunately, though, the actual models passed through Weta Digital, where they were photographed and re-created digitally in 3D; while the models themselves do not appear in the movies, their spirit certainly does, along with their craftsman's touch. We would happily have watched the entire Town Hall take shape as a model; as it was, only the base warranted being built. The structure was later redesigned – more than once as it turned out – as a fully digital model.

The route of Bard's desperate scramble across the rooftops of Lake-town was initially visualized in the form of a modest and very precise model as well, before becoming a dedicated set. The fire that destroyed the digital model was of course entirely digital as well; the original Lake-town model is safely in storage, along with the model of Dale in its heyday.

John Howe, Concept Art Director

MSJ/GB
AD

We built a set that was just rooftops for Bard to scramble over. I did a drawing that we built from, with a nice variety of heights, levels and pitch. The set was reconfigurable so we could change their arrangement and reuse them in different ways to represent new roofs.

Alan Lee, Concept Art Director

LAKE-TOWN CONFLAGRATION

Smaug comes with a force we only commonly associate with the elements – the random rage of storm or wildfire. Here, however, the ravaging elements are driven by revenge and spite, and all the more terrifying for the brutal intelligence that drives them. Smaug knows no human weapon can stop him, nor is he in any particular hurry; like some gigantic feline with tiny terrified mice, he is taking his time.

John Howe, Concept Art Director

JH
WD

MP
WD

MP
WD

Putting myself in the Dragon's place and visualizing how he would make his sweeping passes over Lake-town, I imagined that the devastation would be inflicted in linear rows, like a napalm drop you might see in footage of the war in Vietnam. Perhaps his tail would knock over buildings as he went by as well? Looking at the size of him, any fire coming out of Smaug's mouth would have huge volume. The width of a single burst of flame might conceivably encompass an entire

building, or even several, so he could be flying over the town and incinerate entire streets of buildings with each pass.

In talking with Visual Effects Supervisor R. Christopher White, what we thought would be interesting would be to provide a sense of scale and consequence by putting tiny people in the wide imagery of the attack as well, such as a family huddled on a balcony or the roof of their house,

silhouetted against the flames. The thought was to catch glimpses of little human moments going on amid all the epic ruin, showing how people were trying to get away from the fire and remind the audience both of the sheer scale of Smaug's attack and also the cost of it; humanizing the action.

Michael Pangrazio, Weta Digital Senior Art Director

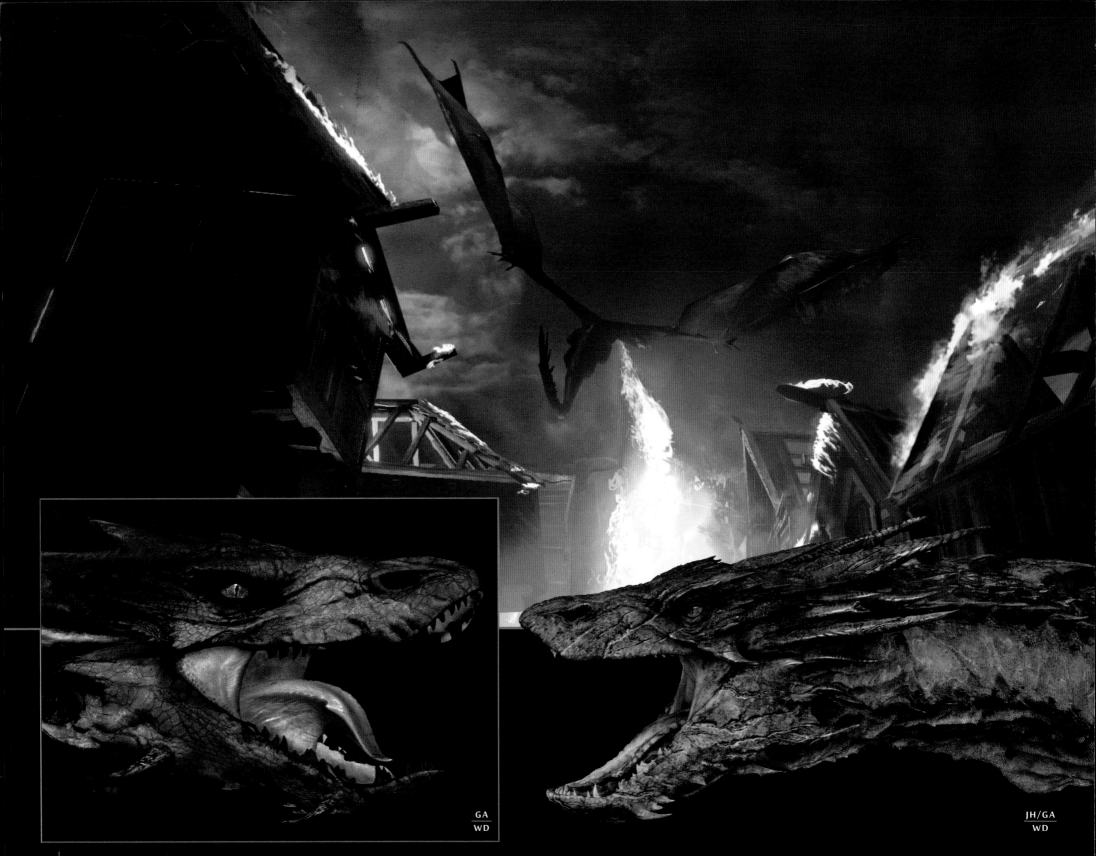

GA
WD

JH/GA
WD

BARD

COSTUME

In the third film Bard has stepped up a notch and taken on the mantle of a leader of his people. It seemed appropriate that this change would be reflected in his costume, so he got a new coat. Somewhere in a cupboard or vault amid the desolation of Dale he finds an old suede coat of blue that he throws over a chain vest of fine rings, a nod to his ancestor Girion's armour.

In terms of cut there was some similarity between Bard's new and old jackets, both being of similar length and silhouette because we wanted to preserve his iconic shape, but the new coat was definitely cut slimmer. The unlined felt coat didn't have the bulk of the fur that his earlier kangaroo skin garment had and swung and spun dramatically when he fought. In his slimmed-down coat Bard very much cut the figure of a long, lean fighting machine.

We also gave the coat a bit of a Tibetan feel. There was thin leather binding on the edge that was similar to the little pointed Tibetan detail of Girion's costume, a subtle link back to his heritage as a descendent of the Lord of Dale and another Eastern influence in our costume design that matched the Eastern influences in the architecture. It would have been a very lush coat once upon a time. There were prints on the cuffs around the hem but we ended up taking them off because they were too strong. Nonetheless, there was a residue of them that could still be seen and it implied that this was once a much more heavily embellished garment, a rich coat, fit for a lord but which had been sitting around in a cupboard for a hundred years or more, gathering dust. Its quality was not obvious or advertised in flashy decoration, but was there nonetheless, a bit like Bard himself.

Bob Buck, Costume Designer

One of the first concepts I did for *The Hobbit*, years and years ago now, was a fairly loose piece depicting Bard, dressed for battle as a king. We had very little idea yet of how the character would be played so it was a stab in the dark and quite an Anglo-Saxon take on Bard with a little bit of an Elven influence creeping in. I rationalized that Lake-town had such a close trading relationship with the Elves that there might be some artistic influence that had rubbed off.

Jump to now and it is clear that Bard and Lake-town in general went in a totally different direction, but it was funny to see that he ended up wearing a blue coat, albeit a very different style to the one I first painted.

Paul Tobin, Weta Workshop Designer

Left: Smaug scar configuration concept art.
Far left: Smaug mouth interior concept art.

PT
WW

MP
WD

BB
CD

LAKE-TOWN

THE BELL TOWER

Smaug recognizes the rusty, antiquated wind lance atop the tallest belfry of the Town Hall – and as quickly smashes it with a swipe of his spiked tail. Bard makes his last stand in a bell tower, hoping against hope to achieve what his ancestor Girion could not, but another swipe of the Dragon's tail nearly topples the tower, and snaps his longbow in two.

John Howe, Concept Art Director

Bard's shooting of the fateful arrow at Smaug was always going to be a very important moment in the film, so John Howe and I were conceiving variations on the tower he would climb, and how this scene would play out, for a quite a long period. John's bell tower was chosen, but not before we offered a large number of interesting and diverse alternatives.

Alan Lee, Concept Art Director

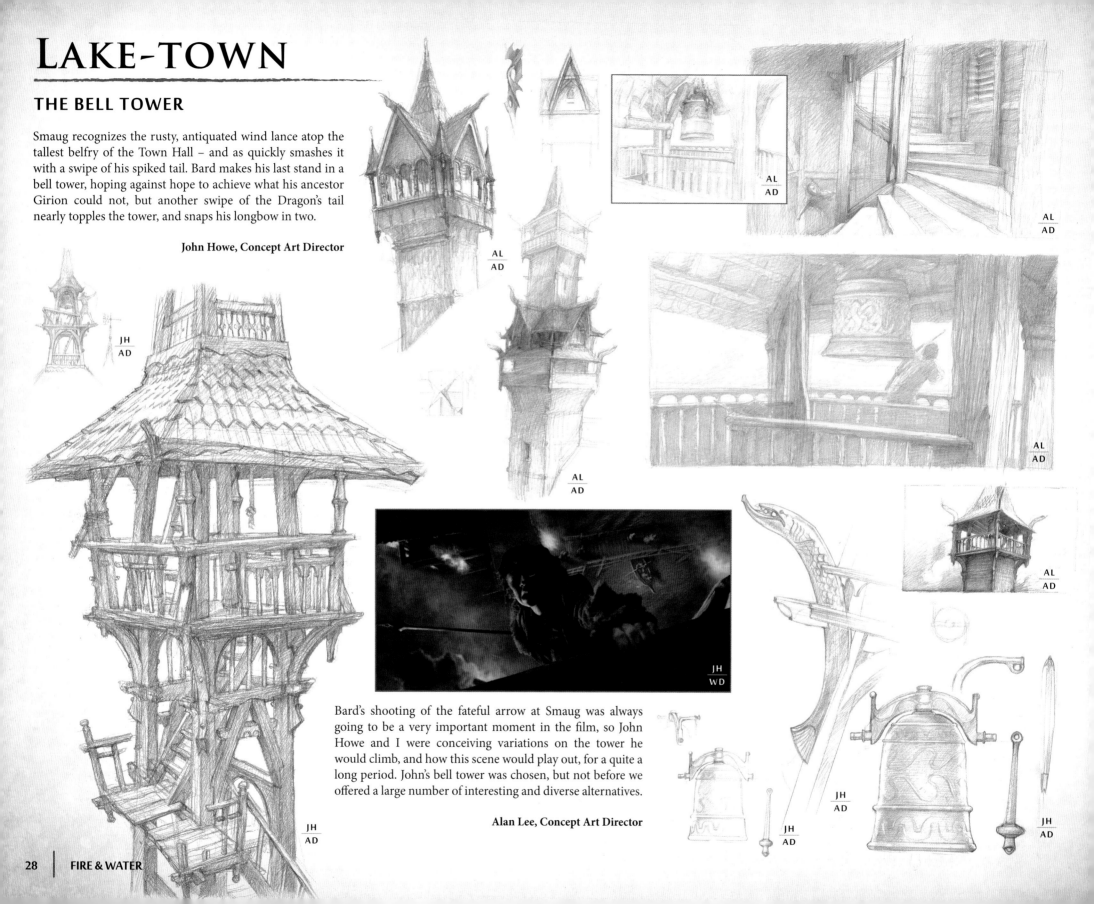

THE DEATH OF SMAUG

Peter's idea for how the Black Arrow would actually be flung at Smaug was quite an interesting one. It required a machine the size of the wind lance that we created for Dale to realistically throw such a huge projectile, but then, with the wind lance destroyed, how would Bard save the town? It required some ingenuity from Bard in the form of a *William Tell* sort of moment with Bain, but was something Peter was very keen on.

Alan Lee, Concept Art Director

Undeterred by a broken bow in his hands, Bard jams the broken ends into splintered beams of his faltering bell tower and draws the Black Arrow with both hands, the shaft resting on the shoulder of his son Bain.

John Howe, Concept Art Director

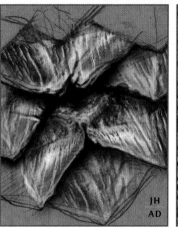

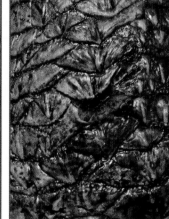

ESGAROTH REFUGEE CAMP

The 5,000 residents of Lake-town are forced to take to the water when Smaug attacks and incinerates their homes. As the town burns the surviving residents cling to what flotsam there is and are blown to the lake shore, where they erect makeshift shelters from the debris of their town. The lucky ones have made it in small boats and rafts which they have pulled up onto the rocky shore. The scene is one of devastation where mothers are trying to comfort their traumatized children and everyone is looking for someone to blame. Fires are giving off smoke as townsfolk try to keep warm and cook what little food they have salvaged from the wreckage. They are a desperate group sheltering from the elements in tents made of burnt timbers and stained blankets, dwarfed by the vast and unfriendly winter landscape that surrounds them.

Dan Hennah, Production Designer

Prop Master Nick Weir came in one day and said, 'Who wants to draw very fast?' Mat Hunkin and I put our hands up, clocked off what we were doing and threw ourselves into a round of furious refugee camp drawings for Nick. The idea was that the people had washed ashore and used whatever bits and pieces of floating debris from the town to construct makeshift shelter. The Lake-town set had just been struck, so the back lot was full of pieces of the set – ladders, stairs, bits of wharf, all tipped over and lying about – so we went over and sketched details of them to reconfigure for the lakeshore campsite. We wanted to preserve some continuity so I would even choose exact pieces and cut them out of the set plans. We drew for as long as we could. It became a little bit of a drawing competition between us! Together we turned out quite a body of work. It was very cool to see the dressed location later and realize that we had drawn all of these chunks of dressing. The whole bank was covered in them. It looked incredible.

Matt Smith, Prop Designer

LAKE-TOWN MILITIA

COSTUME & ARMOUR

The poor Lake-town refugees are washed ashore after their town is destroyed. They're in a sorry state. What they have escaped with is all they have left so they must collect themselves and pull themselves back together, wrapping up as best they can in the cold climate. They also have to arm themselves so they grab whatever they can from the debris of the town to turn into weapons and armour. Household items are repurposed and mixed with bits of boats and buildings or the odd spare bit of Lake-town guard armour to create makeshift shields and protection. They get very resourceful though the result is more a desperate militia than an army. Among the ranks are Lake-town guards who still have their uniforms and civilians who have appropriated or adapted their helmets, gorgets or gauntlets until there's very little distinction. Everyone is pulling together to survive.

Bob Buck, Costume Designer

While the Master would have his regimental guards, the Lake-town soldiery are more of a militia than a standing army so we thought it would be interesting if they were less conventionally armoured. We always hope to offer something that hasn't been seen before and some cultures have made use of materials like hemp, flax or other rope-like fibre to weave armour. Given the people of Lake-town were boatmen and fishermen we thought it made sense they might put their skills in rope-making to use to construct armour, fashioning it quickly and with whatever they had at hand. Along similar lines we also played with scaly fish-skin armour made from the dried skins of large, plated fish.

Paul Tobin, Weta Workshop Designer

I was very pleased with the Lake-town guards I had designed, but felt something was missing. They needed to look a bit more dangerous, so I added the gorget.

Frank Victoria, Weta Workshop Designer

LAKE-TOWN MILITIA

WEAPONS

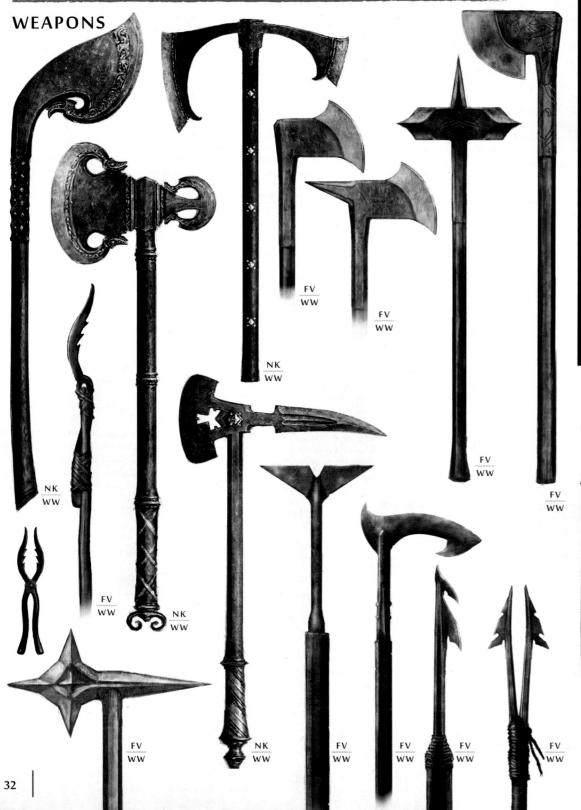

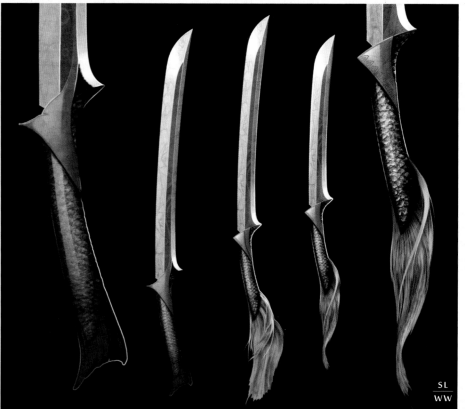

FV / WW

FV / WW

NK / WW

FV / WW

FV / WW

NK / WW

FV / WW

NK / WW

FV / WW

NK / WW

FV / WW

FV / WW

FV / WW

FV / WW

SL / WW

JH / AD

JH / AD

Lake-town is, as we know, a fishing culture, not a warrior nation. The people there would not have a set of weapons ready to go and do battle. But they would have utensils for fishing, and tools for boat or household repair. Using cues from the real world I designed a series of possible machetes and the like.

Frank Victoria, Weta Workshop Designer

I had just been in a pet store and seen some Siamese fighting fish when the brief came through for Lake-town weapons. I loved the idea that perhaps the swords had ornamental tassels or tails, as some Chinese swords did, and I used the fish tails I had been looking at as inspiration. It gave them a softness as well as some colour, and the idea of scaled fish-skin handles as an alternative to leather grips was another chance to do something a little different with a potentially attractive shine and texture. Likewise, I thought perhaps tempering the blade in a slightly different way, using drips of water rather than clay might give a fresh and interesting effect (*inset, above*).

Stephen Lambert, Weta Workshop Designer

The Lake-town weaponry was an exciting brief. One idea we explored was that these weapons once belonged to an ancient culture predating Lake-town as it was now. I used a lot of curves and a crescent moon shape in my designs, creating clear silhouettes that we had not seen before in any of our other Middle-earth cultures. The design process was very fast: we created as many ideas as we could in a day or so, then the approved weapons were built from those sketches. There was no time for refining them further, so the very first concept sketches had to be good enough for someone to build from. The hero Dwarves ended up with a number of these as well. I was particularly happy to see Dwalin use the crescent moon mace at the end of the second film.

Frank Victoria, Weta Workshop Designer

Most of the Lake-town weapons were based on big fleshing knives used in fishing and whaling, but equally as effective as both weapon and tool.

The final Lake-town guards' sword has a hilt wrapped in fish skin with a little decorative fish head on it. Where we could, we introduced the fish motif into their gear in much the same way the horse was everywhere in Rohan. Blue was a colour we saw the Art Department using a lot in their conceptual models of the Lake-town buildings so we adopted it in our work as well, along with the scale motif. We mirrored the rooftops of Lake-town in our hilt shapes and other architecture-inspired decorative shapes.

Paul Tobin, Weta Workshop Designer

DUNGEONS DEEP

DOL GULDUR, LAIR OF THE NECROMANCER

Far from the pyre of Lake-town, amid the strangling thorns and decay of Mirkwood, lies the haunted fortress of Dol Guldur, den of the sinister Necromancer. A hiding place for massing Orc legions, the dank maze of tunnels and crumbling staircases is now a prison to Gandalf the Grey. Entering the grisly dungeons on a suspicion, the Wizard uncovered an army preparing to be unleashed upon the world of Middle-earth, assembled and directed by the disembodied will of none other than the ancient enemy, Sauron, a discovery that would cost Gandalf his freedom.

Hung in a spiked gibbet to watch while the thralls of Sauron march to make war upon his friends, all seems lost for Gandalf, but for the promise that should he ever need her, the lady of Lorien, the Elf queen Galadriel, would be at his side. So it is that in his darkest hour bare footfalls herald the coming of hope, a pure and fragile light, small in the oppressive gloom of the Necromancer's benighted lair, but unbreakable in resolve and righteous dignity. Galadriel has come to Dol Guldur to cast open the pit and reveal the power of the White Council in its wrath.

The battle of Dol Guldur was an opportunity for the filmmakers to depict the war between Middle-earth's principals in a way not seen before, a magical, spiritual confrontation of the world's most powerful beings. While it would have a physical component, with swords clashing and staves swinging, the battle would also be spectral and thematic, hope set against despair, sincerity versus malice, light battling dark, rich imagery for the trilogy's artists to paint with.

DOL GULDUR

We know little of Dol Guldur, but have a hunch that it might well be Númenórean, like so many of the vast and long-abandoned edifices of Middle-earth (Alan and I hid away hints of Númenórean architecture throughout the landscape of *The Lord of the Rings*). Whoever the original builders were, it is a Gothic interpretation of Gothic, upheld by high-pointed arches and built according to a triangular plan – nothing but acute angles and uncomfortable proportions.

On top of this already uninviting structure, the current landlord has done nothing to improve the atmosphere, binding the stones in a criss-cross latticework of metal, imprisoning the crumbling masonry in a jagged fist of rusted iron. Even doing the drawings gave us the shivers.

John Howe, Concept Art Director

Naturally the castle brooding atop the Hill of Sorcery is vast. Only a few portions were built as sets: a causeway and a gatehouse, a cloistered terrace half-crumbled away, a meandering stair leading down to a network of prison corridors and a ruined tower crowned with twisted trees where Gandalf is imprisoned in his iron cage. The sets were already large enough to fill the biggest sound stage, but the digital Dol Guldur was unimaginably bigger. It truly was a digital environment built under a spell of concealment – even wide views only reveal parts of it.

John Howe, Concept Art Director

It's always good to have a plan, but you also have to go in knowing that plan is going to change if it doesn't give the director exactly what he needs. You have to be ready to change with it. It is one thing to know that there is an objective and reasoning behind the arrangements of scenes and sets that allows you to follow characters' progress through an environment like Dol Guldur, but it has to give Peter the shots he wants. Peter is all about the shot. He is unconcerned about whether there is an internal logic to the way certain locations relate to each other as long as when he shoots them they serve his story. That said, having a plan helps get us underway from a conceptual and construction point of view, so we began with an overall idea of where certain sets were in relation to others in the imaginary environment. We could rationalize how the spaces related and how Gandalf would move through them as he penetrated Dol Guldur's levels. It helped us figure out what we had to build, how many of particular elements we needed for specific shots, et cetera.

We had several sets depicting the various parts of Dol Guldur. One was the area outside the dungeon where Thrain is first encountered, while another began as a tunnel running into a labyrinth of passages and cells. There was the forecourt set where Radagast has his tussle with the Ringwraith in the first film, a very nice, compact little set. Additionally we had the dungeon, dungeon interior, south tower and main courtyard. The sequence at the end of the second film, in which Gandalf is pursued after having uncovered the true nature of the place as a hideout for Azog and his cronies, saw quite a small set built for the bridge area where he confronted Sauron.

The modularity of it all meant we could reconfigure and re-dress when we needed to, and a layout being based on a triangle turned out to be a very nice thing as far as shot compositions were concerned. The camera's field of view is essentially triangular, so we had created sets that worked perfectly for the widescreen format.

Alan Lee, Concept Art Director

In Dol Guldur every angle is awkward: the stairs are V-shaped and terribly steep, the silhouettes grim and strangely proportioned, but above all, the whole structure is criss-crossed with bands of rusted iron riveted to the stone and studded with spikes. Even the vegetation, twisted dry vines and tortured trees, reveals in its structure the corruption of the Necromancer. Half of the castle itself has fallen away, exposing the endless caverns and dungeons hollowed out of the hill itself.

John Howe, Concept Art Director

Dol Guldur was a treacherous environment with spikes and thorns, broken stairways, ledges and drop-offs that John Howe and Alan Lee had drawn, a great place for a dramatic pursuit. At one point there was going to be a chase through the place involving Radagast, Gandalf and some Orcs dragging a captured Beorn. In my artwork I tried to push the height of the space as much as possible, so that the bottom often couldn't be seen. I would also layer lots of stairways and platforms going back into the distance so there was a real sense of it being a deep maze, with every corner being somewhere a person could fall or hurt themselves. It's full of ways to die, which makes the chase more exciting.

Gus Hunter, Weta Workshop Designer

Funny story – I had created a background image that I had intended only to use as a backdrop behind the main action, some texture in the background (*facing page*), in a different piece of production artwork (*facing page, inset, bottom*). It was an Escher-esque combination of chunks of Erebor set imagery, an unfinished element that was never meant to be seen on its own, but quite by accident it actually got sent to Peter. To my surprise he singled it out and said that he really liked it! I can look with some pride at the finished film and notice how similar some of the fading background views of Dol Guldur are to that lucky piece.

Anthony Allan, Concept Artist

AA
AD

AL
AD

AA
AD

AA
AD

AA
AD

AL
AD

AL
AD

AL
AD

AL
AD

AL
WD

JH
WD

DOL GULDUR

GANDALF CAPTURED

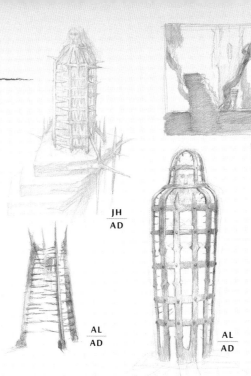

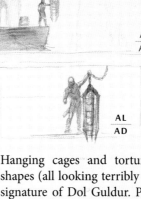

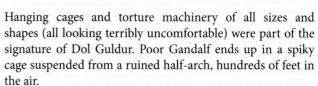

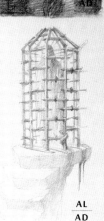

Gandalf penetrates the gloom of Dol Guldur, lighting it up with his staff and peeling back the layers of magical concealment that lie over the old fortress. As he goes deeper he is jumped on by Thrain, Thorin's father, who has been lost for decades and has gone mad. Eventually Gandalf is caught by the Necromancer, revealed to be Sauron, and hung in a gibbet.

Alan Lee, Concept Art Director

Hanging cages and torture machinery of all sizes and shapes (all looking terribly uncomfortable) were part of the signature of Dol Guldur. Poor Gandalf ends up in a spiky cage suspended from a ruined half-arch, hundreds of feet in the air.

John Howe, Concept Art Director

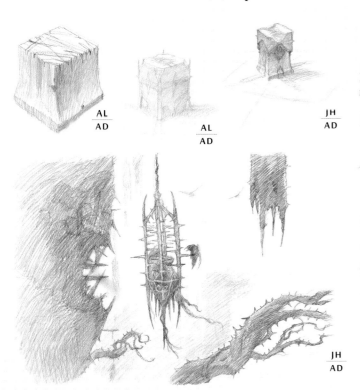

DOL GULDUR

COURTYARD

It's looking grim for Gandalf until the White Council turns up: Galadriel, Elrond, Saruman and Radagast. It's at this point that they learn who it truly is that they're fighting and what is at stake.

Dan Hennah, Production Designer

The courtyard in Dol Guldur became the setting for the White Council's confrontation with the Dark Lord, adjoining which was the south tower where Gandalf was suspended in his cage.

The entire plan of the courtyard was based on a series of triangles with staircases leading up from it, down which the Nazgûl would descend. This triangular geometry was reflected throughout Dol Guldur. We built it in modular units that could be reconfigured within a triangular matrix. We had three towers joined with bridges. They were at different heights and radiated from each other. Turning the units could make them appear to be different, so we were able to achieve a reconfigurable set with a lot of detail that appeared much larger and more rambling than it truly was, which would otherwise have been incredibly daunting.

Alan Lee, Concept Art Director

The White Council takes the fight to the Necromancer, dispelling any notion that these are distant commanders spinning their webs of influence from the safety of their havens and strongholds. As Tolkien wrote of the events of the First and Second Ages, these are figures from an age of heroes, who govern with wisdom, but do not quail from physical combat. They also suspect the Necromancer's true identity, and know that only they have the power to defeat him – if they survive. It is truly revealing of the life of Galadriel, who appears in Tolkien's tales of the history of Middle-earth in circumstances far more perilous than the glades of Caras Galadhon.

John Howe, Concept Art Director

Alan had designed the set for the Dol Guldur courtyard in which the White Council confronts the Necromancer, and the Art Department's model makers had created a maquette of it using foam core board and polystyrene. Peter wanted to see what it would look like in a painting so I went down to talk with Alan and the team there and photograph the model. I stitched together panoramic pictures, then painted over the top, adding colour, lighting and finally the figures of the White Council and Nazgûl battling in that space.

This battle wasn't the same as a regular fight. It had to have a supernatural quality to it because the characters involved were all magical, so part of my task was to explore different effects. If Elrond cut a Ringwraith, what did that look like? Was there a flame effect, or some kind of magical mist, or blood? I played with fire and various glowing effects, offering as many options as possible for Peter to choose from.

Gus Hunter, Weta Workshop Designer

We created a set with staircases running down into the courtyard, down which the Nazgûl would descend to surround the heroes. The battle ensued and the Ringwraiths were knocked into the cracks and crevasses. It was a very different battle to any we had seen before in these films because these were all magical beings with great power. It took place on a totally different level, and there was a lot of nice posturing going on.

Dan Hennah, Production Designer

Initially we thought that perhaps the White Council might have some soldiers with them during their invasion of Dol Guldur, leading me to play with adding some elements, including a full face helmet, to the previously seen Lothlórien Elf armour (*below, right*). I thought we might even see Celeborn in a platinum-silver version, but Peter felt it was important that this be a very different kind of battle and not the sort that required infantry, an astute choice and one that avoided repeating the kind of giant battle we had seen at Helm's Deep, Minas Tirith or Azanulbizar.

We offered up ideas for how the confrontation might play out. Azog was going to be there to harvest Gandalf's Ring of Power. Philippa talked to us about Galadriel protecting herself and the prone Wizard from Azog through the power of her Elven Ring, Nenya, which would manifest flashes of fallen Elven heroes like Gil-galad or Eärendil whenever he tried to strike her. He couldn't touch her.

Daniel Falconer, Weta Workshop Designer

ELROND

It is always difficult to fit something beautiful beneath armour and combine the two gracefully, but I think Elrond's Dol Guldur costume worked very well in the end. I particularly liked that the gold hues of the cuirass and fabric matched in a pleasing way. I hadn't really used such a colour combination before, but Elrond contrasted well with the others in the scene, and with the rust and dark stone of the set. There were a few principals on screen together in the Dol Guldur scenes. I find it is best for each to have a very clear and distinct individuality.

Ann Maskrey, Costume Designer

GALADRIEL

My first concepts for Galadriel put her in armour based on the Lothlórien soldiers, but with bigger, exaggerated shapes in an effort to make a bold statement, more of an icon than something functional (*inset above, far left*).

Paul Tobin, Weta Workshop Designer

When word came to us that we would see the coming of Galadriel to Dol Guldur, something I have long imagined in my own head, I couldn't wait to start drawing. I thought of her in brilliant gold leafmaille like feathers, with golden leaves woven into her cascade of hair, imagining her arrival in the dungeons as being like a dazzling sunrise, untouchable and searing, so bright she burned the eyes to look upon.

Daniel Falconer, Weta Workshop Designer

To illustrate Galadriel's descent into Dol Guldur, and how the environment actually started to affect her, we looked for transformative opportunities in the ideas we were suggesting for her costume. I played with the idea that the pattern-work on her clothing might actually start to take on a thorn-like appearance as Dol Guldur began to infect her. Daniel Falconer and I both played with a colour change, darkening her and in so doing drawing attention to the brightness of her Ring, suggesting perhaps that its magic was at some level affecting the change. My work took the form of gestural studies rather than finished costume designs, meant to inspire and suggest ideas or effects.

Paul Tobin, Weta Workshop Designer

As the script took shape the manner of Galadriel's rescue of Gandalf in Dol Guldur became clear. Philippa described how Galadriel would enter the dungeons barefoot, without armour or escort, looking vulnerable and yet burning with radiant energy. She also described how Galadriel would change (*above*).

I thought of all the thorns and dark energy around the Lady of Lórien, imagining how her raiment might be clawed and torn with dark veining beginning to criss-cross her skin. Yet she would remain unreachable, leading to what Philippa called her drowned look (*left*). To my delight Peter, Fran and Philippa liked it.

Daniel Falconer, Weta Workshop Designer

Galadriel's costume would become ragged from passing through this avenue of thorns, but the idea was that whilst her clothing was torn she was in fact becoming more powerful in a way, absorbing this energy swirling around her in something akin to what Frodo witnessed happening to her in *The Lord of the Rings*.

Alan Lee, Concept Art Director

Several ideas had been put forward for Galadriel's Dol Guldur look. Ultimately her costumes evolved into something with a very simple cut, but were many-layered with a combination of silk chiffons and silk satins. Both fabrics move beautifully, as does Cate Blanchett. I particularly loved a shot Peter composed of her entering through a gate in Dol Guldur, softly treading through the leaves and debris, with the pale blue-white and silvery-greys of her first costume rippling around her bare feet.

Ann Maskrey, Costume Designer

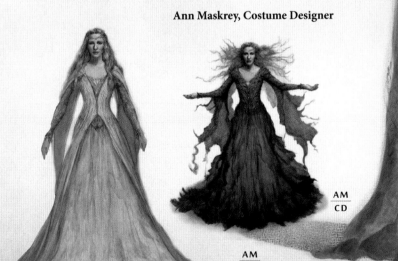

It was essential that Galadriel remained ethereal, and inspiration for both her costumes came to me from the ballet *Ondine*. The second, darker of her costumes (*above*), representing her transformation, had a seaweed feel to it with all the lacey tendrils, through which many other strips of fabrics were twisted and knotted.

Ann Maskrey, Costume Designer

THE NAZGÛL

The Necromancer had summoned his Ringwraiths to him in Dol Guldur. For their appearance in this film Peter asked us to think about a slightly different look for them than what we saw in *The Lord of the Rings*. Perhaps their costuming would look more like what they were buried in, and perhaps they might all carry signature weapons rather than swords. That also gave us the chance to put a bit more of their native culture into their looks. By the time of *The Lord of the Rings* they were more uniform and ethereal, whereas we thought that here was the opportunity to make them more individual.

Andrew Baker, Weta Workshop Designer

I pictured the Nazgûl as something like undead warrior-priests, so I thought it might be interesting to explore the priest angle with some concepts, with habit-like robes of black and white (*facing page, bottom left*).

Daniel Falconer, Weta Workshop Designer

One of the things about the Black Riders of *The Lord of the Rings* was that they were all very much the same. It was only in *The Return of the King* that we saw the Witch-king in a unique armour, so as we had the chance to offer up a slightly different take on them in this film I thought it afforded us an opportunity to make them stand out a bit as individuals and hint at their diverse cultural backgrounds. Apart from Angmar, Tolkien was vague about exactly which kingdoms they reigned over when they were men, but there was the tantalizing mention of a character called Khamûl the Easterling, second in command, which gave us licence to imagine distinct cultural signatures that might show in armour elements worn by the various Ringwraiths during their fight with the White Council. A few of us picked up on that idea and ran with it.

Paul Tobin, Weta Workshop Designer

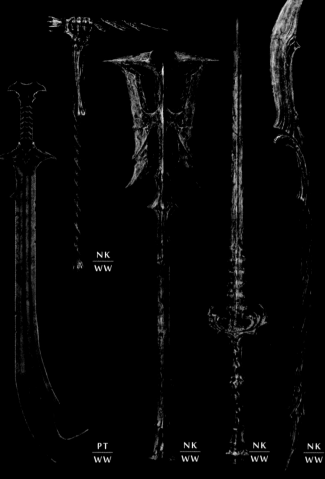

The Ringwraiths were all kings of different cultures so I thought it would be interesting to see some elements in their look that suggested they came from unexplored parts of Middle-earth, places we hadn't yet seen in terms of motifs and shapes. There was also the notion of seeing them in spectral and physical forms and what the differences might be. Even though there is no physical body to see, maybe this time they might wear physical armour over their robes, something brought up from the crypts. Seen with the Wraith-world vision of a Ringbearer they might have beards or trailing long hair (*inset*).

Rather than just swords, it was fun to try out concepts for other weapons for the Ringwraiths, like glaives, picks and war-hammers.

Nick Keller, Weta Workshop Designer

I imagined that the still-immaterial Eye of Sauron serves to guide the Ringwraiths, and that as a symbol of their enslavement to the darkness, their helmets would have no eyes or faces (*below*).

John Howe, Concept Art Director

I imagined the Ringwraiths' approach and attack might be a sort of grim ballet, with black blades held out horizontally and heads bowed (I would so love to hear them chanting as they come), in keeping with the solemn rage that the Necromancer feels at having the fight carried to his very stronghold. Then the battle would explode into a grim dance of death with Elrond, Galadriel and Saruman. They would be dressed in their funereal vestments – long flowing robes heavy with embroidery and decayed finery, and clad in their forge-black armour.

John Howe, Concept Art Director

Peter let us explore some quite diverse looks for the Ringwraiths. I played with how different we could potentially make them in a series of pictures focussing on their armour. For simplicity's sake, I approached the design by depicting them without any spectral qualities, as they might have appeared physically. It was still unclear at this stage how spiritual or physical they would be in the final film, so removing this element from the artwork meant we could see the materials and shapes of the armour to start with and think about what the ghostly effects might be later.

The notion of them all being kings from different lands inspired me to push them each in different directions and make them unique rather than an army of nine identical beings. There were some similarities with real cultures from our own world, but I didn't base any of them on any one historical race we might recognize – it was more an exercise in trying out different shapes and combining different elements like plate and chain to various degrees. Some were almost entirely plate-armoured, while others wore more scale or chain. I was looking for unique silhouettes for each character

so they could be easily picked out from the others, and that included finding distinct helmet shapes and different kinds of weapons rather than just swords. I thought it would be interesting to give at least one of them an armoured mask on his helmet that had a representation of a human face, complete with a beard of chain. It wasn't something we had seen before in Middle-earth.

Nick Keller, Weta Workshop Designer

AL
AD

NK
WW

NK
WW

THE NECROMANCER

The most challenging characters to design in any film are often the ones that are more ethereal than solid. Exactly what the Necromancer would be was an open question with many possible answers. It required the impressive illustrative skills of Gus Hunter to finally nail this character for us, though some great options were pitched by everyone, ranging from creatures to humanoid voids to something smoky and spiritual, and of course, the fiery red Eye.

Richard Taylor,
Weta Workshop Design & Special Effects Supervisor

GH
WW

AJB
WW

DF
WW

AJB WW   AJB WW

GH
WW

Peter's brief to us for the Necromancer was something like a black hole, a vaguely Sauron-shaped silhouette, sucking in all life and light. We imagined that, when he interacted in a scene with Galadriel, there might be a recognizable event horizon where his magic is met by the opposing force of the Elf queen's power.

Another alternate look we explored was something perhaps a little bit more like the Ringwraiths as we saw them when Frodo was wearing the Ring. It was what he might have looked like underneath the armour we saw him wearing in *The Lord of the Rings*: a demonic, physical presence.

Andrew Baker, Weta Workshop Designer

I liked the idea that perhaps the periphery of the hole that was Sauron was a mist of screaming, anguished faces.

Daniel Falconer, Weta Workshop Designer

GH
WW

One of the directions we explored with the Necromancer had him like a void in space, sucking everything in like a black hole. Peter wanted to see what that was like. The whole environment was shrinking into this humanoid-shaped void as he moved through it.

In the early days of the design we had worked up a number of Necromancer ideas, including some that were hazy silhouettes composed of black, inky smoke. Matty Rodgers painted a close-up of the head in which he included the flaming cat-slit Eye that people would recognize from *The Lord of the Rings* (*overleaf, bottom right*), because Sauron, as we find out, is the Necromancer. Peter quite liked that idea, though he didn't necessarily want to see the Eye exactly, but perhaps something suggestive of it. We came back to this concept again, later in the process, which led to me doing

a new round of paintings showing possible different stages as the effect changed (*overleaf*). We had wind blowing the smoky effects around, exposing what look like bones inside him. There's the hint of a human shape in there when it starts. The wisps get bigger and swirl around and you can see this eye-like thing burning where his head should be, recalling the Eye on Barad-dûr, but different, so it's a link to the other films but not the exact same thing repeated. Peter liked the idea of light piercing through the head, creating the impression of something like an eye, but wanted to also see how that might give us some kind of mouth to play with as well, because we were probably going to see him speaking.

Gus Hunter, Weta Workshop Designer

The notion of a smoky Necromancer with shapes that looked like bones, lit up from inside, was something that came up very early in the project. We set it to one side but Peter came back to the idea and asked for it to be developed further. Peter wanted to see that it wasn't just smoke, but that there were arms with hands, and something like a mouth that could talk, so we would see the Necromancer, Sauron, actually speak with moving lips. I explored variations of how that might appear, with the Eye of Sauron, which audiences would recognize, being part of the face.

GH
WW

GH
WW

MR
WW

The Necromancer's final reveal as Sauron in *The Desolation of Smaug* came when Gandalf went to Dol Guldur. There was all kinds of smoke-and-mirrors magic happening in Dol Guldur. The Orcs could come in and out of it, protected by the illusion that the Necromancer had created. Gandalf didn't know where they were until they began coming out of the walls, so the artwork I created was supposed to be very creepy and forbidding.

Gus Hunter, Weta Workshop Designer

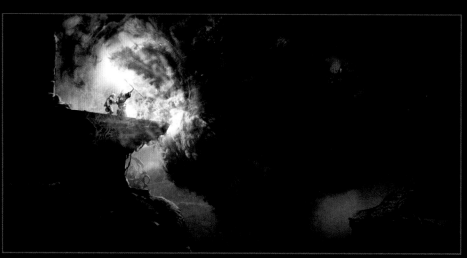

GH
WW

The Necromancer started as a smoky black, inky cloud, but then became a fireball. Peter wasn't sure what that was going to look like so he asked me to have a go at working up some options. As the effect happens the fireball becomes something like a burning eye, the Eye of Sauron from *The Lord of the Rings* and the cat-slit pupil then becomes the figure of Sauron in his armour. Gandalf tries to defend himself with his staff, creating a kind of force-field effect around himself, but Sauron's power in his fortress is too great and Gandalf is eventually overcome. Gandalf is thrown back against the wall. Thrain was part of the scene when this artwork was done and he is sucked into Sauron at that moment. The Necromancer then reveals himself as Sauron in ball of flame.

Gus Hunter, Weta Workshop Designer

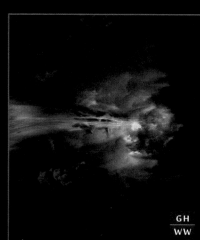

GH
WW

GANDALF'S VISION

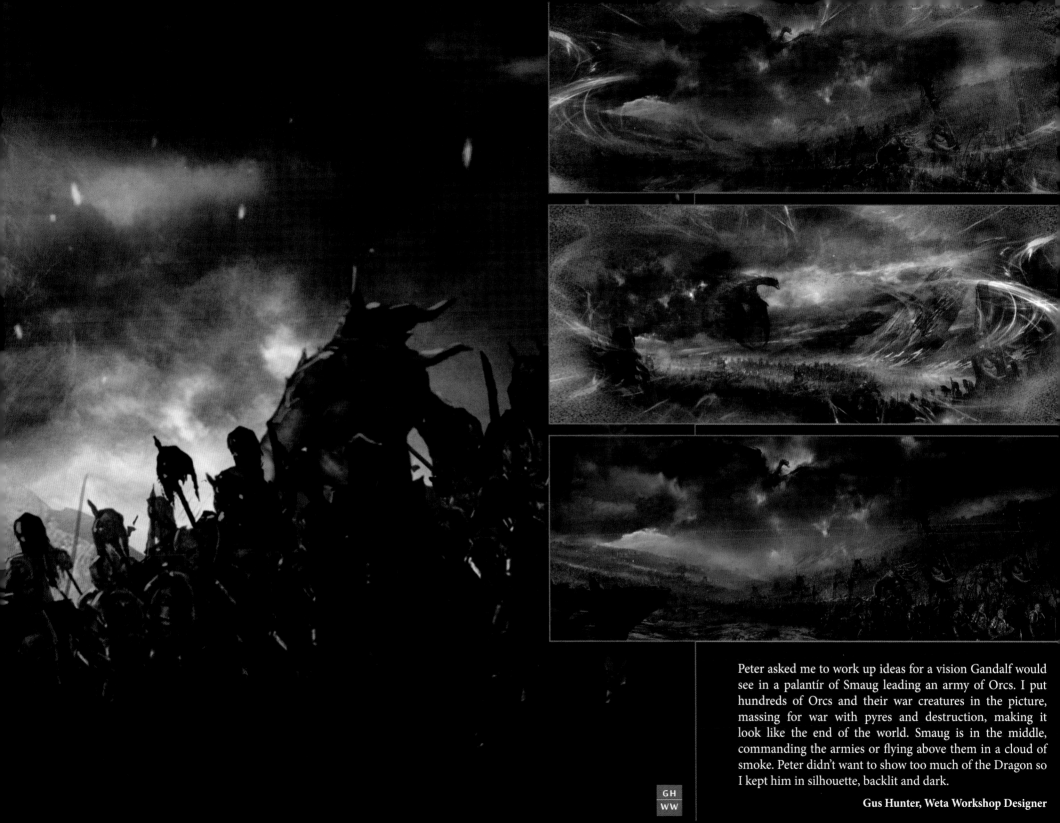

Peter asked me to work up ideas for a vision Gandalf would see in a palantír of Smaug leading an army of Orcs. I put hundreds of Orcs and their war creatures in the picture, massing for war with pyres and destruction, making it look like the end of the world. Smaug is in the middle, commanding the armies or flying above them in a cloud of smoke. Peter didn't want to show too much of the Dragon so I kept him in silhouette, backlit and dark.

Gus Hunter, Weta Workshop Designer

GH
WW

GH
WW

AL
AD

DOL GULDUR

ESCAPE

As we shot it, the escape from Dol Guldur had Gandalf still quite badly wounded, being evacuated from Dol Guldur by Radagast on his sledge. There was a pursuit through the castle ruin with its broken staircases and bridges, a perilous chase culminating in them bursting out of the fortress's crumbling lower levels and into the forest again at ground level. At one time Beorn was going to be present, a captive of the Orcs. It was an opportunity for Radagast to show some heroics.

Alan Lee, Concept Art Director

AL
AD

RADAGAST

STAFF

Gandalf's staff was lost when he was taken by the Necromancer, but Radagast gives his friend his own when they part company after the rescue in Dol Guldur.

Alan Lee, Concept Art Director

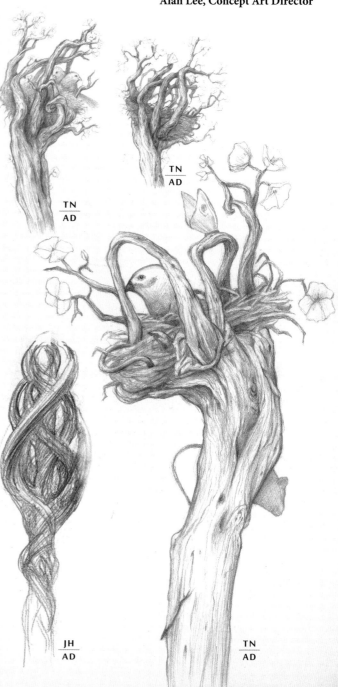

TN
AD

TN
AD

TN
AD

JH
AD

TN
AD

As it turns out, this is the staff that Gandalf still carries in the beginning of *The Lord of the Rings*, so that design came first. When we came to design Radagast's staff we worked backwards from Gandalf's, created twelve years earlier. We imagined that some of the knotty roots on the head of Gandalf's rod had perhaps been longer once and more tangled, a bit like Radagast himself. Sculptor Anneke Bester took a casting of the original prop and made additions. Radagast would also carry a crystal in his version where Gandalf would later insert his pipe. We thought about putting a bird's nest in it, but that ended up in Radagast's hair instead.

Alan Lee, Concept Art Director

CAVERNS OLD

EREBOR, KINGDOM OF THE DWARVES

Home to the Dwarves of Durin's line and object of the quest of Thorin Oakenshield and his Company, Erebor was once a kingdom teeming with people and treasure, the richest of Middle-earth's realms and famed and coveted in equal measure. Having driven the Dragon from his hoard, Thorin and his fellow Dwarves set about reclaiming their kingdom, ordering its vast riches and shoring up its defences for the challenge they know will come; for a treasure such as this, left unguarded …

Erebor was not the first deserted Dwarf city the filmmakers and their conceptual crews had created for the Middle-earth film trilogies. In *The Lord of the Rings* the Fellowship had passed through what remained of Moria, like Erebor a mine and city carved deep into the rock with yawning chasms and vast, abyss-spanning bridges and stairways. But the kingdom beneath the Lonely Mountain had to be distinct from Moria, which also appeared, briefly, in the prologue sequence of *The Hobbit*'s first chapter, *An Unexpected Journey*. While still unmistakably

Dwarven with its hard, faceted surfaces, squared-off archways and eschewing of rounded forms, Erebor had its own unique stylistic departures. Where Moria had been brown or grey in hue, Erebor was depicted cutting through glossy green marble shot with gold-laden quartz. *The Hobbit* is replete with cavernous underground kingdoms, but the halls and atria of Thorin's home would be as characteristically Dwarven and singularly original as Thranduil's subterranean empire was so unmistakably Elven, or the Goblin King's pitted fiefdom a den of Goblin debauchery and abuse.

Like Moria, Erebor and its treasure hoard would be depicted through a combination of live-action sets and props, as well as digital environments and extensions; though unlike Moria of the previous trilogy there would be no shooting of miniatures employed, as 3D filming rendered model effects impractical in this instance.

Erebor
CAVERNS & HALLS

Erebor's green palette helped set it apart from Moria, the Dwarf realm we visited in *The Lord of the Rings*, which was more brown. The inspiration came from a beautiful Chinese marble, flecked with rusty gold. We theorized that the entire Mountain was a giant chunk of green marble with veins of quartz running through it, into which the Dwarves had tunnelled, following the gold in the quartz formations. There is a Russian salt mine in Poland in which generations of miners did more than just extract salt; from the living rock they mined they carved chapels in which to pray. The walls were carved into the most extraordinary galleries of sculptural art. We imagined our Dwarves to be like those miners. Dwarves are craftsmen by nature and cannot help but carve things of stately beauty, so as they followed the seams of gold into the heart of the Mountain they expanded their tunnels into halls and living areas with pillars, staircases and statues. Some of the vast quantities of gold that was mined was put to use creating balustrades and fixtures, so the entire space was rich and polished.

Dan Hennah, Production Designer

In the prologue, Erebor was described as the 'greatest kingdom of Middle-earth', so it certainly had to be grand and spectacular. Like the other underground kingdoms – Goblin-town and the Woodland Realm – what was built on stage was a tiny portion of the final realm, even though the biggest of the sets filled the largest of our sound stages. Peter was far less concerned with the inner logic of the spaces, but determined that each should feel vast, varied and complex.

Now, though, the gleaming and polished halls of Erebor are dark and cold as a tomb, the only fire and warmth remaining there is in the belly of the deadly wyrm.

John Howe, Concept Art Director

One of the first pieces I produced on *The Hobbit* was an architectural study for Erebor in pen and ink (*below*). I had been looking at art by Escher for inspiration and Alan Lee's Dwarven architecture from the previous films. We were looking at everything from ancient European ruins to Indian designs. John Howe hit on something very strong with his work which was almost like hanging architecture.

Anthony Allan, Concept Artist

Statues seemed to come naturally into the monumental scale of Erebor, underling the fact that the Dwarves hardly see themselves as dwarfish. The colossal statues of kings, the figured columns with their axe-bearing atlantids supporting the vaults of Erebor all speak for the sturdy and enduring nobility of the Dwarvish race.

John Howe, Concept Art Director

Dwarven architecture is characterized by cavernous spaces with lots of pillars. There was an Art Deco influence in the shapes; lots of hard, strong lines, angular motifs and diagonals.

Dan Hennah, Production Designer

JH
AD

Peter was very clear about wanting Erebor to have a lot of height, so the spaces inside the Mountain were not only expansive in terms of halls that faded into the distance, but also with amazing depth.

Anthony Allan, Concept Artist

Erebor's carved architecture is dominated by mega monoliths. Having been created by the Dwarves following the quartz veins, the underground city is a labyrinth of interconnected halls and arcades with stairs and flying bridges on multiple levels, weaving through the cracks and crevasses in the living rock of the Mountain. Light filters down from cracks high above in the Mountain's surface and lends an eerie glow to the depths. The architecture is embellished with inlays of gold and precious stones, with balustrades and chandeliers made from precious metals.

Dan Hennah, Production Designer

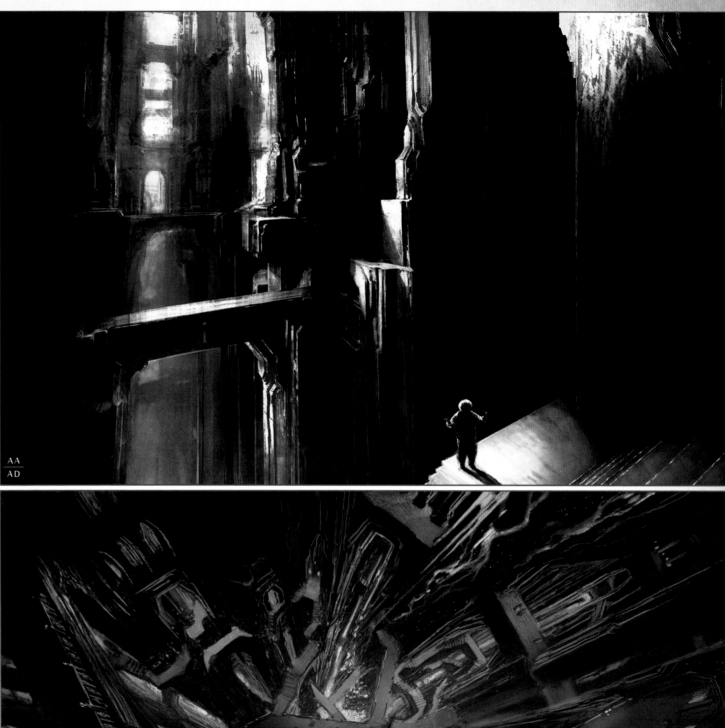

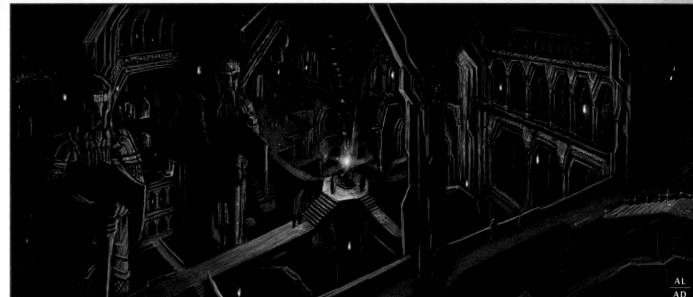

EREBOR

THRONE ROOM

The throne of the kings of Erebor is the base of a natural column of rock suspended from the vaulted ceiling of the throne room, thickly veined with gold and carved to seat the king. The Arkenstone is set above the seat, but no longer in our early concept art – Smaug's great talons have rent the stone itself when he sought to tear the glowing gem from its mounting. Originally, the elaborate gilded gate to the treasure halls was situated directly behind the throne.

John Howe, Concept Art Director

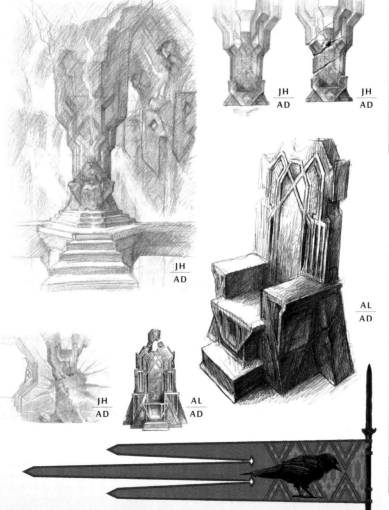

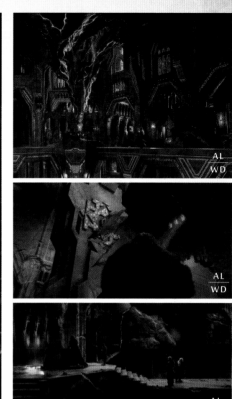

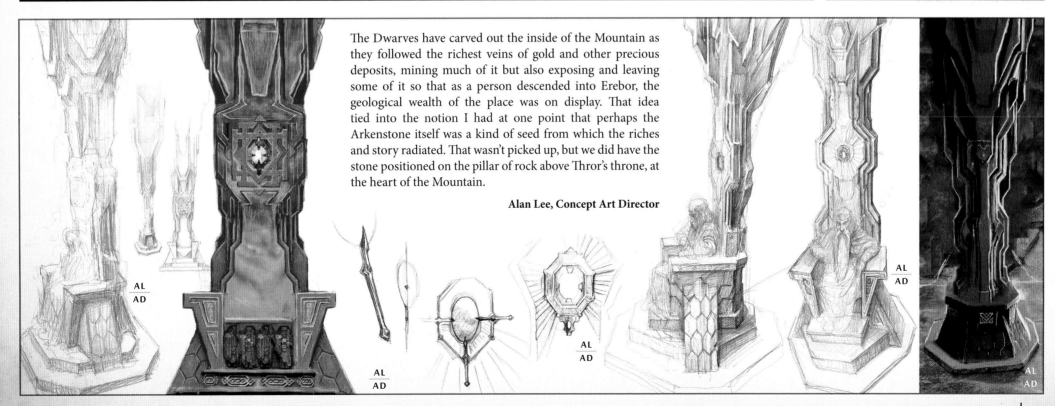

The Dwarves have carved out the inside of the Mountain as they followed the richest veins of gold and other precious deposits, mining much of it but also exposing and leaving some of it so that as a person descended into Erebor, the geological wealth of the place was on display. That idea tied into the notion I had at one point that perhaps the Arkenstone itself was a kind of seed from which the riches and story radiated. That wasn't picked up, but we did have the stone positioned on the pillar of rock above Thror's throne, at the heart of the Mountain.

Alan Lee, Concept Art Director

THE TREASURE OF EREBOR

The treasure we built was probably 50/50 drawing based and a case of props workshop crew making things up. We bought a lot of raw and cut stones from Swarovski for our team to use. The coins went through a full design process, and we created a large selection of designs for things like goblets, for instance, that we could both replicate as they appeared in the drawings and also mix and match, swapping interchangeable parts to make them look different. We didn't just want a sea of coins. It was important that the treasure hoard be filled with lots of other things as well, anything that we could come up with that could pass as treasure, so there were candelabras, trays and plates, mirrors and all sorts.

Nick Weir, Prop Master

Amid the treasure of Erebor was a set of gems that the Dwarves had set into silver for Thranduil, the Lasgalen jewels. They are part of the reason for the enmity between Thranduil and the Dwarves. It can be a challenge to conceive of something which has to possess an aura of preciousness that has to hold such importance for the characters. There is a lot for the design and props to live up to, but I enjoyed drawing these (*facing page, lower left*) and was very pleased with how well the final props turned out.

Alan Lee, Concept Art Director

silver
pearls
diamonds
sapphire
emeralds

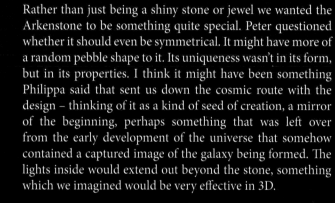

THE ARKENSTONE

Rather than just being a shiny stone or jewel we wanted the Arkenstone to be something quite special. Peter questioned whether it should even be symmetrical. It might have more of a random pebble shape to it. Its uniqueness wasn't in its form, but in its properties. I think it might have been something Philippa said that sent us down the cosmic route with the design – thinking of it as a kind of seed of creation, a mirror of the beginning, perhaps something that was left over from the early development of the universe that somehow contained a captured image of the galaxy being formed. The lights inside would extend out beyond the stone, something which we imagined would be very effective in 3D.

Alan Lee, Concept Art Director

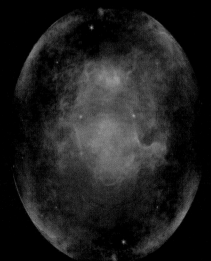

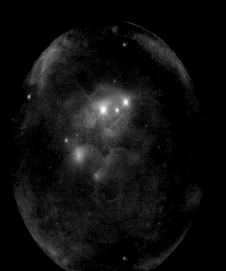

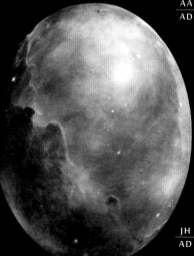

AL / AD

AL / AD

AL / AD

JH / AD

AL / AD

EREBOR

COUNTING ROOM

Filled with huge columns of carefully stacked coins, boxes of jewels and treasures beyond description, the counting room has lifting booms and winches to help with the task of ordering and inventorying the vast treasure that Thorin's team have reclaimed from Smaug. The volume of treasure they have to sort is monumental. Thorin's new kingdom is peerless in wealth, but all the King under the Mountain can think about is the whereabouts of the Arkenstone…

Dan Hennah, Production Designer

AL / AD

Smaug's treasure hoard is an untidy mattress of jumbled gold of every sort: coins, statues, shields... comfortable only for a Dragon, and a far cry from the orderly treasure halls of Thror. Naturally, the Dwarves – being Dwarves – begin counting and assessing their treasure, and of course searching for the Arkenstone that Thorin so covets to affirm his kingship and assuage the greed that eats at his soul.

John Howe, Concept Art Director

The counting room was a fairly small set that would need to be digitally extended to match the true scope and grandeur that Peter imagined. It was a rich set with its stacks of treasure being accounted in an orderly fashion.

One of the issues with the counting room set was how to handle the coins. I came up with a design for stacking them in a visually interesting way, whereby the Dwarves would offset each row that they stacked in pillars, creating a spiralling texture that almost looked like huge coils of golden rope. We created one which was cast and reproduced so that the set dressers didn't have to spend weeks stacking individual coins!

Alan Lee, Concept Art Director

Bombur is the treasure expert of the group, and as such is given the enormous task of compiling a complete manifest of the hoard of Erebor (*far right*). Thorin naturally hopes that this thorough and painstaking exercise will eventually reveal the Arkenstone, since every piece must be examined and catalogued, hall by hall, alcove by alcove. Bombur's manifest gives us a glimpse into the little-known ancestry, history and dynasties of his race, listing items such as 'Golden statuette of Nárin of Nogrod', 'Golden vase with Zirakalin design', 'Statuette of Gwalin III, jade' and 'Necklace of silver and gold, Nogrobar motif'.

Daniel Reeve, Graphic Artist

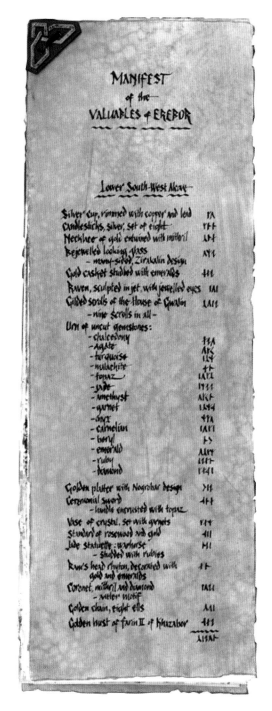

EREBOR

MINES

Erebor's deep mines are centuries old, having been begun by Thorin's ancestors as they mined the quartz veins containing gold and precious jewels in the green marble of the Lonely Mountain. The Dwarves turned their mines into architectural masterpieces and moved into them as they tunnelled, but even in the days of Thror there are still active mines. The Mountain's deep roots hide riches yet to be uncovered.

Dan Hennah, Production Designer

AA
AD

AL
AD

JH
AD

MH
AD

AL
AD

AA
AD

AL
AD

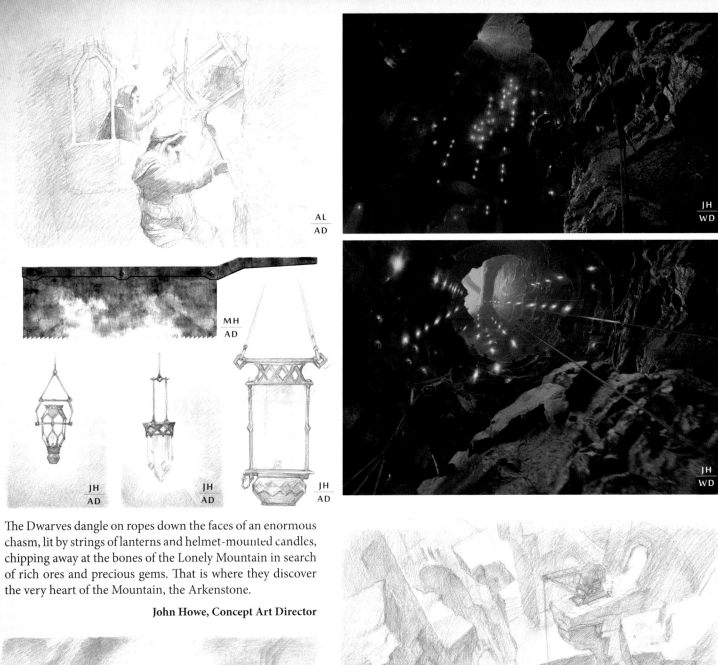

AL
AD

MH
AD

JH
AD

JH
AD

JH
AD

JH
WD

JH
WD

The Dwarves dangle on ropes down the faces of an enormous chasm, lit by strings of lanterns and helmet-mounted candles, chipping away at the bones of the Lonely Mountain in search of rich ores and precious gems. That is where they discover the very heart of the Mountain, the Arkenstone.

John Howe, Concept Art Director

AL
AD

JH
AD

JH
WD

AL / AD

AL / AD

AL / AD

AL / AD

EREBOR

JEWELLERY WORKSHOPS

The Dwarven jewellery workshops of Erebor, deserted by the time Thorin and his Company come back to the Mountain were glimpsed briefly in the first film. I thought the ideas being explored offered us a wonderful contrast in scales, with incredibly fine detail work being carried out by the Dwarves with great big magnifying lenses and all kinds of contraptions, while we also had huge industrial processes going on in the background.

This was where the Dwarves would have set the white gems that Thranduil presumably commissioned them to craft into fine jewellery for him; and where all the jewellery would have been wrought that we would see the merchants selling in Dale and elsewhere.

Alan Lee, Concept Art Director

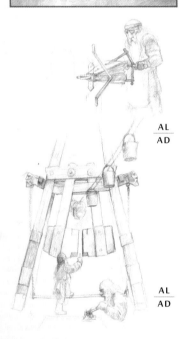

AL / AD

AL / AD

AL / AD

JH / WD

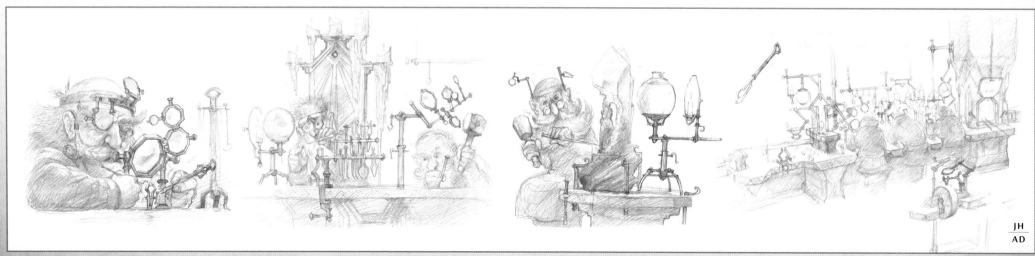

JH / AD

EREBOR

ARMOURY

The armoury of Erebor was untouched by Smaug: a grand amphitheatre lined with thousands of suits of armour and weapons. This is where Thorin's band, who have lost their possessions several times over on their difficult quest, come to don the finest regal armour of the Dwarven realm on the eve of the battle, and where Thorin presents Bilbo with a kingly gift.

John Howe, Concept Art Director

We always want to present a set that is architecturally interesting, but in the case of the armoury the environment really existed in order to show off the armour. The design challenge was more a question of how best to display the suits and weapons.

Alan Lee, Concept Art Director

EREBOR

FRONT GATE

We did many designs for the front of Erebor. This was not some discreet fortress with a gate hidden from view: the Dwarves have carved the Mountain itself into a glorious façade that displays their skill and power. Nevertheless, it is a fortress, with battlements, machicolations and a defensive moat. Yet it is no defence against the Dragon Smaug, who smashes the two-foot-thick oaken iron-bound doors and bursts through the wall itself.

John Howe, Concept Art Director

One of the first environments we had the chance to play with was the Front Gate outside of Erebor. The giant statues on either side of the doorway were part of the concept from the very beginning so the artwork we did explored how they would be positioned – standing, sitting, crouching, identical or mirror images of each other, and what the style of the sculpture would be. They had to be epic in scale and imposing. With Peter it's always about being epic!

Gus Hunter, Weta Workshop Designer

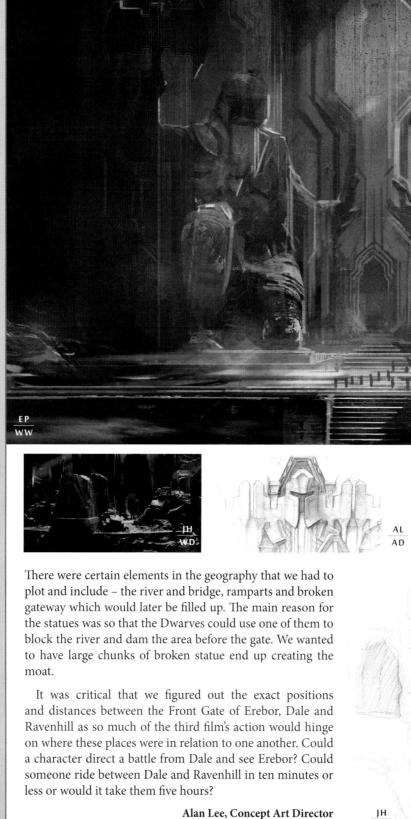

There were certain elements in the geography that we had to plot and include – the river and bridge, ramparts and broken gateway which would later be filled up. The main reason for the statues was so that the Dwarves could use one of them to block the river and dam the area before the gate. We wanted to have large chunks of broken statue end up creating the moat.

It was critical that we figured out the exact positions and distances between the Front Gate of Erebor, Dale and Ravenhill as so much of the third film's action would hinge on where these places were in relation to one another. Could a character direct a battle from Dale and see Erebor? Could someone ride between Dale and Ravenhill in ten minutes or less or would it take them five hours?

Alan Lee, Concept Art Director

AL
WD

We had to think carefully about the design of the ramparts, firstly for Smaug's attack and then again for when the Dwarves barred the entrance to the Mountain, turning the creek into a defensive lake. One of the concepts we explored was the notion that Smaug had toppled one of the giant statues guarding the gate, damming the flow of the water and creating a pool in front of the entrance.

Alan Lee, Concept Art Director

AL
AD

JH
AD

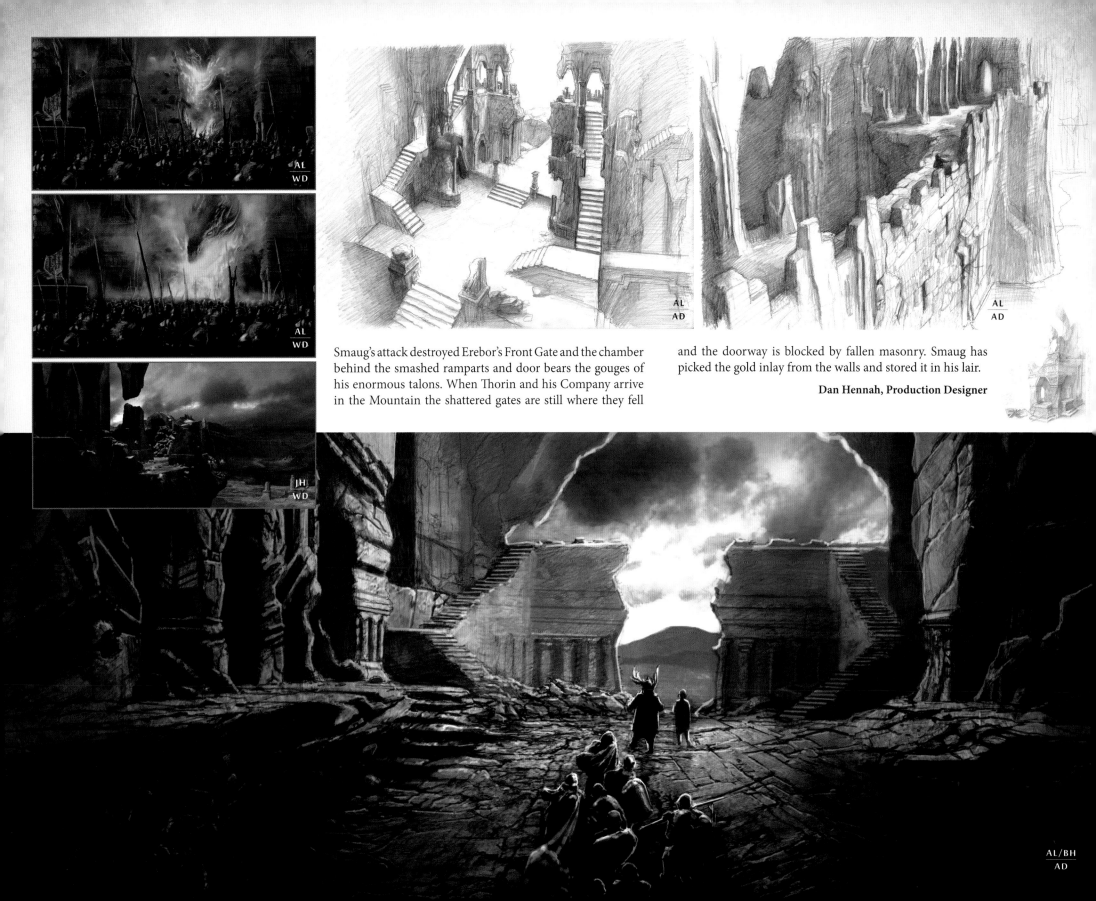

Smaug's attack destroyed Erebor's Front Gate and the chamber behind the smashed ramparts and door bears the gouges of his enormous talons. When Thorin and his Company arrive in the Mountain the shattered gates are still where they fell and the doorway is blocked by fallen masonry. Smaug has picked the gold inlay from the walls and stored it in his lair.

Dan Hennah, Production Designer

JH
AD

AA
AD

JH
AD

JH
AD

When Smaug swept down from the Withered Heath and destroyed Erebor, the invincible ramparts of the kingdom were brushed aside and destroyed. Smaug's entry into the Kingdom Under the Mountain left the outer wall breached, the bronze-bound oaken doors splintered and shattered, the very stone of the Mountain smashed by his bulk and rent by his claws. With Smaug's death, Thorin and his doughty band would rebuild the ramparts and destroy the bridge to the front entrance. I do regret that Smaug doesn't reserve the same fate for the hidden door, as in the book: I imagined him ravaging the secret Valley of the Dwarven Kings, toppling statues, and burying the back door under a scorched landslide. The Dwarves are master stone-workers. They gather up the shattered pillars of Erebor and weave a wall, interlocking the stones diagonally – strong against the assailant, but with a surprise or two, should they wish to issue forth in a hurry, for they know full well that the demise of the wyrm will bring many beggars to their gate.

Thorin, the king without a kingdom, has reclaimed his halls, and he has no intention of giving them up. The dreamed-for day has arrived, but with it his heart has hardened. So long a homeless vagabond, he has no sympathy for the bedraggled refugees of Lake-town that shelter in the ruined halls and houses of Dale, and even less inclination to deal with Thranduil, at whose feet Thorin lays the blame for decades of bitter errancy. But above all, he has caught the dragon-sickness, like Thórir of the Icelandic *Gull-Thóris* saga; one could imagine him laying on his gold and slowly becoming the *flugdrekar* he so long dreamt of slaying.

The defences Thorin oversees were built in two separate sound stages: the very top with the machicolations, and the Erebor entrance hall itself, but only up to a certain height. The two were stitched together digitally, with a gap of two metres or so made not of painted polystyrene, but of pixels. The sculptors built two versions of the sets, one of Erebor's gleaming and polished heyday, one the claw-scored and devastated Erebor of the Desolation of Smaug, filled with dust and rubble, similar to the 'pre- and post-Smaug' city of Dale.

Naturally, Bilbo's quiet courage provokes an unexpected turn of events, with the hobbit throwing a rope over the ramparts and clambering down both sets (with the help of a digital double who makes the entire descent) and hopping across the debris in the moat before making his way to Dale with the Arkenstone.

John Howe, Concept Art Director

When Bard and his people take shelter in Dale they presume that the Lonely Mountain is deserted: when the Dragon came to destroy Lake-town the Dwarves were presumably already dead. It is a surprise to them, then, when Alfrid spots braziers burning upon the ramparts of the old Dwarf city. It also meant we had Dwarf braziers to design, as well as rationalizing the fortifications the Dwarves had erected which would greet Bard when he sought them out.

Alan Lee, Concept Art Director

The Dwarves, for whom pulleys and levers hold no mysteries, reclaim a great bronze bell that Smaug's passage has torn from its moorings, and suspend it high above their makeshift fortifications. When they release it, the bell swings down, smashing the wall outwards into the besieging Orcs, and rolls off down the battlefield, sonorously crushing anyone too slow to get out of its way.

John Howe, Concept Art Director

Thorin and his Company come out of the Mountain to join the battle and we wanted to give them a grand entrance. The idea of a giant bell inside Erebor being used like a battering ram to bust through the wall gave us a great way for them to join the fight. We came up with the idea that maybe Dain was about to be pummelled by Orcs when he is saved by the debris of the doorway being blasted out and landing on them.

Gus Hunter, Weta Workshop Designer

JH
AD

EREBOR

THORIN'S TOMB

In the deepest roots of the Lonely Mountain the crypt where Thorin, Fili and Kili are laid to rest was conceived as a kind of amphitheatre where mourners could gather and look down upon the tombs. We were seeking a very mournful and sombre atmosphere, carried through with the lighting, but also a sense of grandeur provided by the giant Dwarven figures supporting the plateau upon which the tombs sat.

Alan Lee, Concept Art Director

AL
AD

AA
AD

JH
AD

AL
AD

AL
AD

JH
WD

AL
AD

MP
WD

AL
AD

AL
AD

AL
AD

DALE,
CITY OF MEN

THE DEFENCE & RUIN OF DALE

Neighbouring the Dwarf-realm of Erebor, the city of Dale was built in the Long Valley between the Lonely Mountain's southernmost arms. Dale was a place of commerce and prosperity, where Dwarves and Men traded and co-existed, welcoming guests from across Middle-earth who came to enjoy its famous markets or conduct business with the Mountain's lords and leaders. It was a bountiful place with fruit trees and plenty, whose people wanted for nothing and enjoyed the friendship of each of the neighbouring kingdoms, be they Dwarf, Man or Elf. When Smaug fell upon Erebor Dale lay in his path and was first to be destroyed. In truth the Dragon had little interest in the city, his prize being the famed treasure of the Mountain.

In the Dragon's wake the town was left a ruin, scorched and smashed, its people fled and its markets and gardens abandoned. Winter reclaimed the barren streets and Smaug's presence ensured the lands surrounding it remained a waste, named ever after by the survivors the Desolation of Smaug. Many took up residence in Lake-town, among them the descendants of Girion, Lord of Dale, whose Black Arrow knocked a single scale from Smaug's flank but failed to kill the beast.

It was not until the reclamation of Erebor by Thorin that Dale was repopulated, but it was no joyful return. In cruel symmetry, it was refugees from Lake-town, made homeless by the Dragon's fresh attack, who would make the long, cold trek and seek shelter in the blasted walls of the old city. Built with fortifications, Dale would be defended again, this time from Azog and his murderous Orc horde, sent by the Necromancer to make war upon the North.

The filmmakers depicted Dale in both its pristine condition and ruined state, with design influences flowing in both directions to shape the city. As a ruin, Dale had to play stage to much of the battle that would dominate the final film of the trilogy. It took shape as a massive outdoor set built on a hillside overlooking the city of Wellington, but was also digitally extended and at times entirely digital. The set was built and shot in its pre-ruined state to begin with and then re-dressed and distressed for the battle scenes.

ANCIENT DALE IN FLAMES

Dale was the garden city of Middle-earth and a trading centre where the Dwarves of neighbouring Erebor soldtheir toys and jewellery. It was a thriving city full of well-fed, happy, safe people as spring turned into summer on market day when Smaug attacked. Smaug's coming was like a nuclear apocalypse, sending superheated blasts of flame that cooked the residents, coating them in a cast of ash. Silhouettes of people running were burnt into the city walls. The city guards sounded the alarm horns to prepare to fight but were no match for Smaug. Bard's ancestor, Girion, loosed numerous six-foot-long black arrows at Smaug but only succeeded in dislodging one scale.

Dan Hennah, Production Designer

Smaug's attack on Dale is a storm of fire, whipped by his vast wings. I imagined it might be at dawn, with mist filling the valley, soon to be replaced by the smoke of the burning city.

John Howe, Concept Art Director

These drawings (*right*) were not storyboards as such, but a sequence showing an idea for the destruction of Dale and Girion's failed attempt to fight back. The idea of the larger crossbow with its giant black arrows came from Peter.

Alan Lee, Concept Art Director

JH
AD

AL
AD

I wanted to take a snapshot of the carnage in Dale, to create an image that was a frozen moment in what was going to be a very dramatic and fast-paced action sequence. Smaug would be moving very quickly and the idea was that the sequence would be more of a tease than a full reveal of the Dragon. At the time we didn't have a Dragon design yet, so I didn't want to get bogged down in trying to design him for the sake of the Dale attack artwork. I therefore kept him largely shrouded in smoke and dust and fire, so he was more of an environmental effect in the artwork than a creature design statement. Smaug is busting through buildings like a freight train, creating havoc with his body as much his fire breath. It was all about drama and scale. I wanted to make sure the true scale of the Dragon was clear. These guys on the walls really don't stand a chance against him. It's a scene of total devastation and chaos.

Gus Hunter, Weta Workshop Designer

GIRION

We had to turn around Girion's costume and armour in a very short space of time, so both Weta Workshop and the Costume Department worked on this at the same time. My first designs drew upon the standard Dale soldier, but elevating Girion from the rank and file with decoration and colour. There were also numerous ideas that we had suggested for the soldier that we were able to revisit and offer up for Girion. Peter wanted him to be distinct, so we started pursuing a look that was almost samurai in feel with his purple coat. We used the regal purple as something of an accent colour in the concepts I was working up because it's a colour that often signifies nobility, so he had an air of dignity and stateliness.

Less armour and more costuming emerged as the direction to take him in. We looked at Persian armour and that is where the idea came from of the large gambeson side sleeves, that could perhaps be soft armour rather than rigid plate metal. I thought they gave us a strong and distinguishing shape, almost wing-like, to play with around his shoulders.

Finally, we ended up grabbing a sword that had originally been made for the Master of Lake-town, but which looked like it wasn't going to be used (*original concept art, right*). A quick repaint of the physical prop into the Dale colour scheme and we had a great sword for Girion.

Paul Tobin, Weta Workshop Designer

PT
WW

BB
CD

PT
WW

PT
WW

THE WIND LANCE AND BLACK ARROW

The proportions of Dale's double-bowed ballistae were dictated by the size of the Black Arrow, which was in turn decided by the size of Smaug. Clearly, a normal-sized arrow, even legendary, would not inconvenience the Dragon any more than a mosquito bite. The double bow echoes Renaissance models designed to hurl heavy javelins.

John Howe, Concept Art Director

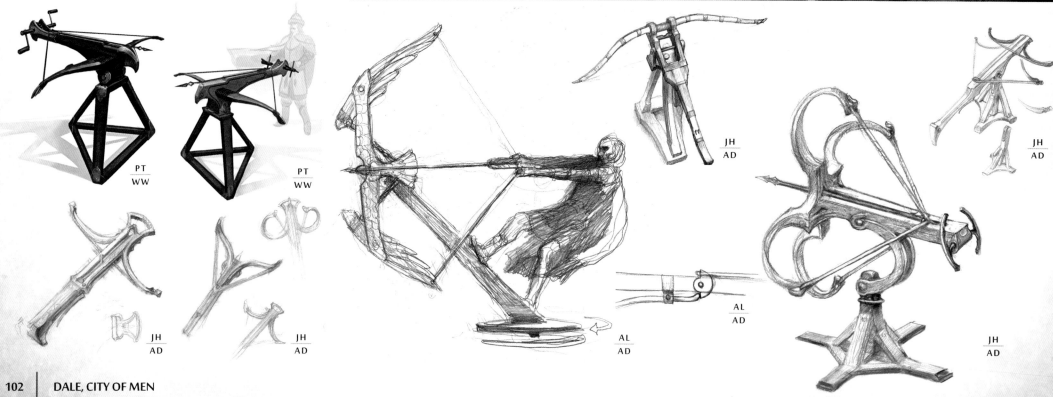

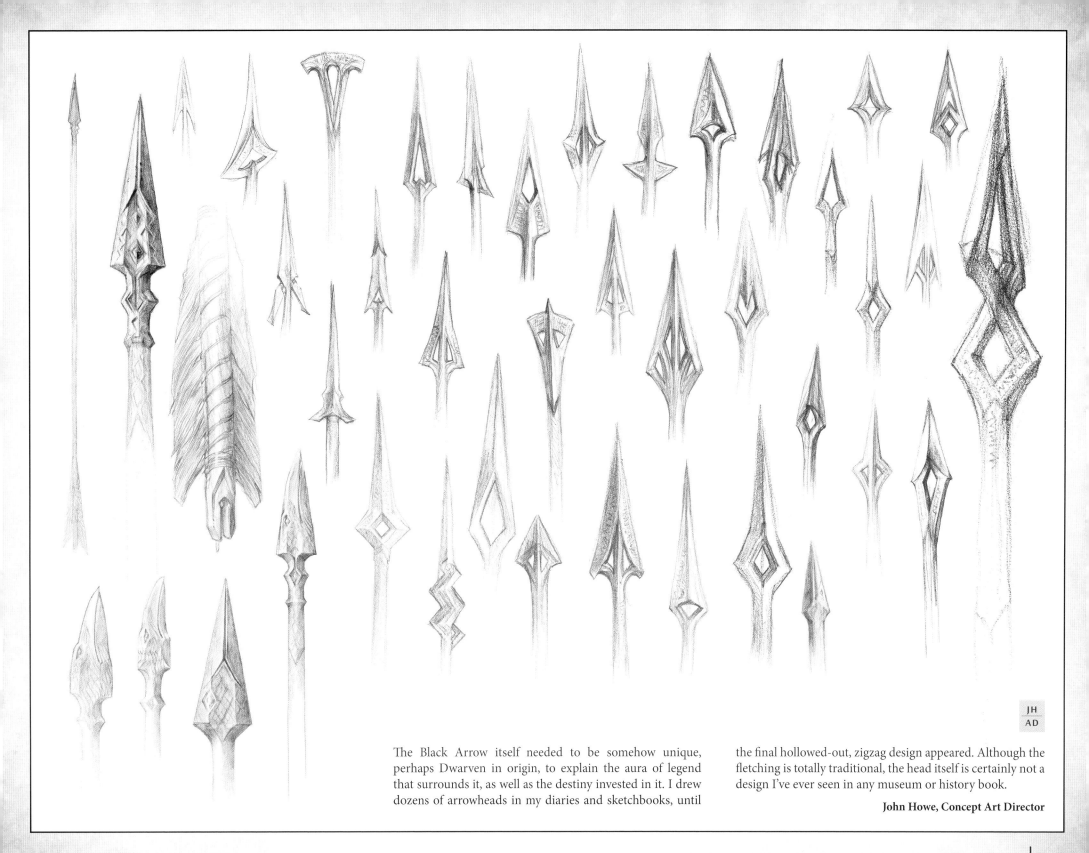

The Black Arrow itself needed to be somehow unique, perhaps Dwarven in origin, to explain the aura of legend that surrounds it, as well as the destiny invested in it. I drew dozens of arrowheads in my diaries and sketchbooks, until the final hollowed-out, zigzag design appeared. Although the fletching is totally traditional, the head itself is certainly not a design I've ever seen in any museum or history book.

John Howe, Concept Art Director

SOLDIERS OF DALE

Thinking about the soldiers of Dale, I was keen to build some kind of relationship to the Rohirrim, because my understanding was that the two cultures might have shared a common heritage. That was one element, but we were also looking at Eastern influences, taking cues from what was happening in the environment designs, and there were elements we found interesting in Tibetan, Mongolian and also some early Russian and Georgian costumes. In Rohan the horse became a dominant icon. I was trying to think of something equivalent for Dale and recalled that birds feature very heavily in *The Hobbit*, and in particular in association with the Lonely Mountain. I began experimenting with bird iconography in the stamped leather and metal elements of the Dale armour, but with little stylistic flicks and curves that pushed the designs further East in flavour. I also sought strong contrast, using highlights of gold over a darker under-colour. The earliest designs had a strong Dwarvish influence as well (*inset, left*), but we dropped that almost immediately as there was already going to be plenty of that in the films.

The helmet design changed quite late in the process from something that was probably too similar in shape to the Gondorian helmets of *The Lord of the Rings* from the front (*facing page, left*) to something fresh. We enhanced the spike atop the helmet and added a band of fur that encircled the head, which also helped align them more with the Lake-town helmets (*facing page, inset*).

Paul Tobin, Weta Workshop Designer

I thought using gold in the weaponry of Dale was a good way to reinforce the prosperity of the culture at every level, right down to the guardsmen on the city ramparts. I also quite liked the idea of pursuing lots of ties rather than buckles, just as another point of difference from the other cultures we had seen in Middle-earth. In a way, what we ended up with in the soldiers of Dale was a kind of fusion of real-world and Middle-earth influences which ended up feeling familiar and believable, even if it was in fact made-up, which is a great place to land with our final designs. They looked like Eurasian Vikings.

Paul Tobin, Weta Workshop Designer

THE RUINS OF DALE

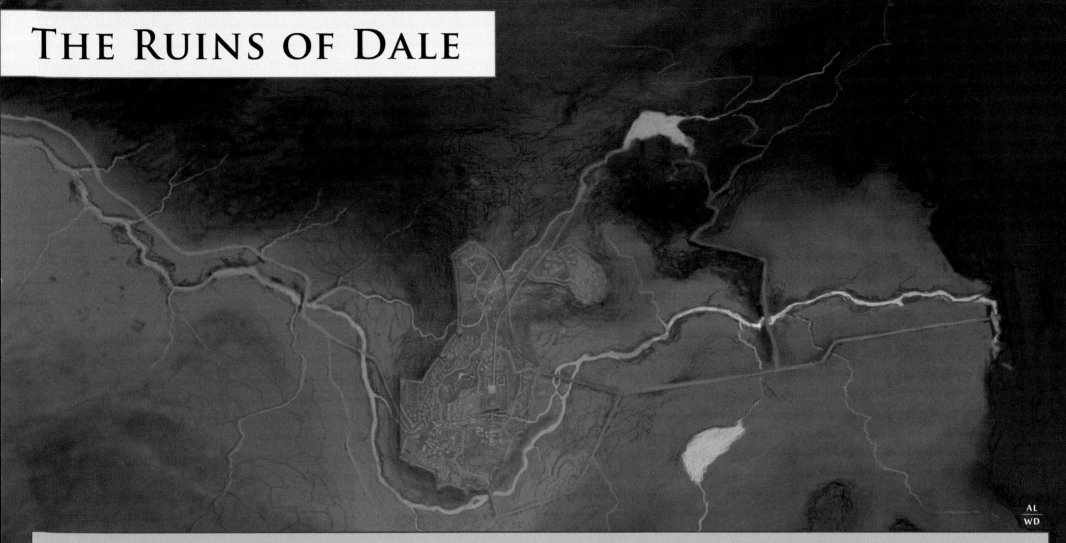

AL
WD

It was very important to establish lines of sight from the main vantage points of the Long Valley, between the ramparts of Erebor and Dale and the fortress of Ravenhill, and from there to situate the Long Lake and the still-smouldering ruins of Esgaroth. The Battle of the Five Armies takes place throughout the length and breadth of the Long Valley: Dain's Iron Hill Dwarves stream over a high saddle from the east; Bolg's Gundabad Orcs swarm over the rocky ridges behind Ravenhill; the refugees from Lake-town defend the ruined ramparts of Dale, where the Elves also take their stand; while Thorin and his doughty little troop must somehow turn the tide when they burst out of Erebor... a very complicated stage to set for the last act.

John Howe, Concept Art Director

AL
AD

water
rock
roofs
paths, roads
walls
set or model

JH
WD

Weta Digital has been doing some very interesting things with the geography of the valley between Erebor and Dale. The technology has opened up some fascinating possibilities. We can now choose almost any area in New Zealand and obtain a 3D image of it down to one-metre square accuracy, which means we can reproduce real, natural geography as digital models by using the DN data. Overlaying photographic textures, it was giving us some very good results.

We also use photo-spacing techniques, whereby some clever software allows us to reproduce a three-dimensional object or environment based on photographs taken from different angles. The computer can interpret the geometry of the object and build it very quickly using only two-dimensional pictures for reference, so, once again, we can create very natural-feeling places.

The tricky bit is knitting these spaces together believably, because there really isn't anywhere in the world that can give us exactly the geography as described by Tolkien for this particular region. The script action demands quite a specific configuration of features in proximity. The area outside the Front Gate of Erebor, including the eastern saddle (down which the Dwarf army rides), the wide bowl of the valley between the arms of the Mountain (in which the battle takes place), and the ice river (leading down towards Dale), together comprise an invented space. It isn't difficult to make little bits of it look great, but building a cohesive, believable geography out of them all was a trickier challenge.

Alan Lee, Concept Art Director

When the Orc armies arrive, the refugees of Lake-town have found shelter in Dale, and stumbled on the armoury abandoned a century and a half earlier. The ragtag army of Lake-towners, reinforced by their grim and determined womenfolk, defends the crumbling ramparts of Dale. They have little hope on the great battleground on the valley floor, where the war-hardened Dwarves and Elves can barely hold their own, but they stand a chance in Dale, relying on ambush and feint, drawing the Orcs away from the battlefield and fighting a stubborn retreat through the steep streets and alleys. Thranduil as well has established his camp high on a terrace in the ruined city, fiercely defended by his Elven archers and warriors.

John Howe, Concept Art Director

Production Designer Dan Hennah was giving me visual cues as far as what architectural styles to look at. My job was to visualize what Dan had in mind. We had begun in a Tibetan or Chinese border world, but as the architecture developed more European influences crept in until we ended up with a blend of familiar influences that was its own thing, something that was grounded in our world but not any one culture that could be pinned down.

Dan had me work quite large on the Dale concepts so that we could print them out on big sheets of poster-sized paper and pin them to our meeting-room wall. The idea was that, if we needed to, we could zoom in very close and still see plenty of detail on individual buildings. Your eye could wander through the streets and levels of the city and explore it within the one picture (*see image, pages 96–7*).

Anthony Allan, Concept Artist

In front of Dale there is a bridge that Bard and Thranduil have a conversation on when Bard returns from his unsuccessful entreaty with Thorin.

The architecture and layout was influenced to some degree by what kind of action the Director wanted to see take place there. Peter was anxious for the battle in Dale not to look too much like a repeat of the siege at Helm's Deep. For that reason we wouldn't see many rows of ladders, for example, but while there would be fighting in the streets, Peter was also keen that the battle not just be a random mess of skirmishes and duels either. He wanted ranks of soldiers and to be able to follow the ebb and flow of the battle from a distance.

Alan Lee, Concept Art Director

MP
WD

MP
WD

JH
WD

JH
WD

AL
WD

AL
WD

DALE, CITY OF MEN | 109

Dale in pre-Dragon times was all about colour, abundance and life. We had paintings and frescoes, trees full of brightly coloured fruit, herbs growing in pots and a market richly dressed with enticing produce and goods. There were toys and jewellery from Erebor for sale, and flying overhead were banners, bunting and kites.

For the scenes set in the city after the Dragon had scorched it and the people had fled, we re-dressed the exact same giant outdoor set, only now in a state of sadness and desolation. We stripped all the joy and colour from the set. The fruit trees were all gone and all that was left of the hanging gardens was ironwork. Here and there sad little reminders of the sudden devastation could still be seen, which just made it all the sadder. Our potter Ivan Vostinar had made thousands of beautifully hand-glazed and stamped tiles for ancient Dale, which were still visible in the burnt and ruined version, glinting in the snow. While part of the contrast between the glory and ruin versions was the removal of all the summery colour, it was important for the desolate city to have its own colour palette and not simply be grey. We researched what happens to rocks heated to high temperature and found that there's actually a kaleidoscope of colour inside the scorch marks on old stones. Beneath the charred surface were purples, pinks and blues, and this research helped set the tone for ruined Dale. We applied these colours to the walls and surfaces, adding soot and scorched detritus, then took it back gradually, seating it in the charcoal, and finally adding the stark contrast of the fresh snow over the top of it all.

The snow was very important to our set dressing because it established visual guides in the set. We used it to trace the outline of a building, guided by the shadows cast by the eaves, or piled it strategically to guide the eye through the set, painting with snow to create contrast where we wanted it. We were advised by the special effects team, but our design for the placement of the snow was done as set decoration and dressing, which is a different mind-set. It was there to complement the set rather than simply blanket it.

Ra Vincent, Set Decorator

DALE

INTERIORS

When the refugees from Lake-town arrive in the ruined city of Dale they seek shelter in some of the city's remaining structures and protected understorey. While there is some fire and water damage, many of the rooms are largely as they were when Smaug attacked. The walls are almost as colourful as they once were, with their rich original palette, influenced by Eastern architecture.

Dan Hennah, Production Designer

DALE

ARMOURY

Deep within the ramparts, the armoury remained untouched by Smaug's sudden devastation, still overflowing with antiquated weapons and armour none of the defenders had time to snatch a century and a half before. This set went from the drawing board to being shot in just a week, one of the quickest sets that was built.

John Howe, Concept Art Director

The tower adjacent to the hall, with its external staircase, was designed with Girion's attempt to fend off Smaug in mind, but Peter felt it would be better to mount wind lances on the hall itself, so they replaced the turrets and we dispensed with the tower altogether.

Alan Lee, Concept Art Director

DALE

GREAT HALL

The design of the great hall of Dale was influenced by looking East. India and Tibet have vaguely similar structures with towers capped in similar ways as well as the wooden-framed windows with decorative surrounds set in stone walls, but we also strived to maintain some classical influence in the hall as well.

Alan Lee, Concept Art Director

AA/AD

AL/AD

AL/AD

AL/WD

Alan Lee had produced some beautiful pencil sketches of a grand hall in Dale, which would have been a seat of government in the city. The design was headed in a good direction and I was asked to create a detailed plan drawing based on the idea. I worked up a very detailed flat view of the building in ink or pencil and showed it to Dan Hennah, who liked it so much he said, 'Great, now let's see what you think it might look like in colour?' That was tricky because I hadn't drawn the hall with any perspective or depth, given it was just intended to be a plan, but I worked back into it, adding some foreground content and painting into the image to try to turn it into a realistic painting.

Anthony Allan, Concept Artist

DALE

THRANDUIL'S TENT & THE REFUGEE CAMP

Our focus on the great hall of Dale was plot driven. It was a vantage point over the city and in the version of the script we were referring to at the time a lot was to happen there, including things taking place before and after Smaug's attack on the city, so we would see it both ruined and pristine. We designed both at the same time, so ideas that looked good in a piece of ruined hall concept art would influence its pre-ruined form, and vice versa.

Early on, Alan created beautiful artwork which didn't necessarily reflect the final design but had a great feel, with crumbling architecture and vines growing through it. We had settled on a domed building with a caved-in roof and two of its four sides demolished, so I worked up a piece and a complementary reverse angle with the intention of bringing that mood into the design we were pursuing. We knew there would be dialogue going on in this location, near what used to be the throne room of the old city, a once-grand place with panoramic views of the valley. Set Designer Mark Stephen modelled architectural elements digitally, which I would grab and arrange to give me a head start in my drawings. As with almost everything on these films, the process was very collaborative.

Anthony Allan, Concept Artist

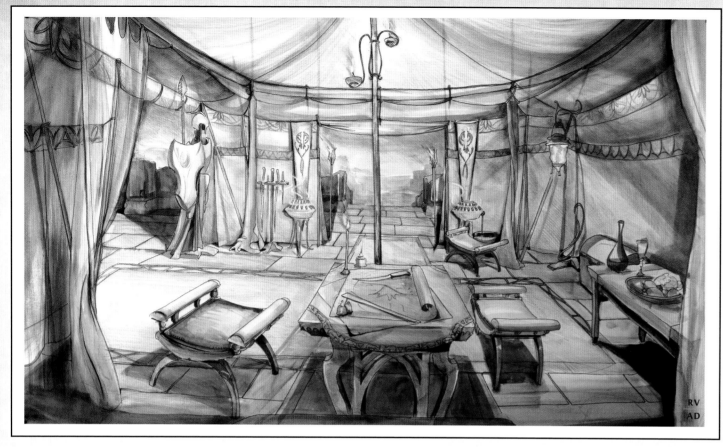

Thranduil sets up his campaign tent in the ruins. Originally this was to be beneath the collapsed dome of the grand hall of Dale, the highest point in the city, affording magnificent views of the whole valley leading up to the Front Gate of Erebor.

Dan Hennah, Production Designer

As the script developed, the refugees of Lake-town came to inhabit what was originally designed to be the great hall and Thranduil's headquarters tent shifted to a promontory overlooking the valley.

John Howe, Concept Art Director

Thranduil's new campsite worked out very well because it afforded us some wonderful views of the battlefield and Erebor. We no longer had to bury his tent within a structure. Now it could be more visible. It also meant the refugees would be sheltering behind the locked doors of the great hall, which made sense.

Alan Lee, Concept Art Director

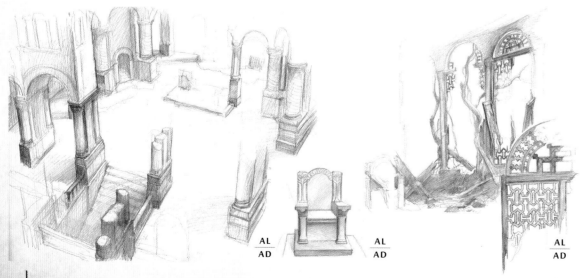

For a time Thorin was going to be slain closer to Dale and the scene in which he would be reconciled with Bilbo before he died was to take place within the ruins of the hall. As the script evolved, Thorin's fate would be decided at Ravenhill instead, where he would fall after fighting Azog and then be carried from the battlefield by Beorn.

Alan Lee, Concept Art Director

THE BATTLE IN DALE

We were coming up with ideas for how the geography of Dale might offer opportunities for some interesting scenarios during the unfolding battle. We figured that the Dwarves were smart enough to use the environment to their advantage, leading some of the huge battle creatures on to the thin ice of the lake near Dale to trap them, or knocking over stone statues to roll over Orcs pursuing them. I liked the idea of a crazy chariot ride through the city's alleyways – the only way to go would be down. Bilbo could be hanging on for dear life while the others swiped Orcs out of the way.

It was winter so perhaps there were sheets of ice hanging from the ruined architecture? Legolas might shoot hanging icicles, releasing sheets of ice to have them fall on the Orcs below.

Gus Hunter, Weta Workshop Designer

An idea was kicked around within our team that perhaps Thranduil and Gloin might have a moment at some point in the battle which was a subtle nod to the friendly rivalry we saw between their sons Legolas and Gimli in *The Lord of the Rings*. Gloin might be about to attack some Orcs when Thranduil comes sweeping through and beheads them, saying something like, 'Keep up, Dwarf'.

Andrew Baker, Weta Workshop Designer

We knew that Alfrid had to meet his demise somewhere in the midst of the battle so we explored how that might happen. One idea, as I imagined it, was something a bit like the Burke situation from *Aliens* in which Paul Reiser's character sacrifices everyone else in order to protect himself, and then, thinking he is safe, actually meets his end rather horribly. Maybe Alfrid would lock himself in somewhere, leaving women and children outside, only to get killed by Orcs that have breached his little bolt-hole.

Peter favoured the idea that Alfrid would somehow find himself in a catapult, getting fired out and into the mouth of some horrible creature. We ended up designing a specific Troll just for that gag, but before we got to that iteration of the idea I suggested a version in which Alfrid would be backed out onto some beam or plank projecting out over a cliff face. Counterbalancing him is an Orc, which Bard might end up shooting with an arrow in an attempt to save Alfrid, but when the Orc topples so does Alfrid's precarious perch and down he goes, onto a Troll captain.

Greg Tozer, Weta Workshop Designer

One idea I had was that in the course of the siege in Dale the defenders cut loose some massive bronze bells from the towers and that these would go careening through the streets, flattening anything in their path and making a hell of a racket. We had seen bell towers in Dale in the first film so it could have perhaps tied nicely together. I thought Alfrid might also end up in one of these, climbing up in there to get away from the Orcs, but the weight of them pursuing him would have pulled the bell free and it had toppled and rolled with Alfrid being pummelled by the giant metal clapper inside.

We were thinking about how to get Bilbo from Dale up to Ravenhill to witness the confrontation going on there. There was quite a distance between the two locations as designed and a river in a steep-sided valley to cross as well. My idea was that Bilbo was pursued and made use of a collapsed tower that had fallen against the bluff bordering Ravenhill during Smaug's assault decades earlier, providing a natural bridging element for the hobbit to clamber across. If it was crumbling away beneath him and his pursuers then it could be a dramatic moment as well as a device to move him from one place to another.

Peter liked the idea, but thought that it was perhaps something that would work better as a location in which Legolas and Bolg would square off, with the remains of the tower crumbling away beneath their feet.

That still left us with the problem of getting Bilbo to Ravenhill, so another concept I pitched involved using a giant waterwheel. In Syria I had seen some enormous waterwheels that were very dramatic. They would be a functional thing that a city like Dale might actually have for drawing water from the river below. This was my Middle-earth version of those Syrian wheels, yet bigger. Once they were moving, all Bilbo would have to do would be to grab a paddle and hold on; there would be all kinds of potential for cool action and peril on a giant waterwheel.

Paul Tobin, Weta Workshop Designer

FLEET-FOOTED ELVES

MIRKWOOD GOES TO WAR

King Thranduil opens the doors of the Woodland Realm and marches his great column of glimmering Elven soldiers east toward the long shadow of the Lonely Mountain. Offering succour to the bedraggled survivors of Lake-town's conflagration, the Elven-king installs his host amid the ruins of Dale and prepares to outlast the Dwarves holed up inside Erebor.

The third Elf army created for the Middle-earth films, the Mirkwood host followed the army of Lothlórien and Last Alliance forces of *The Lord of the Rings*, a legacy that brought with it both benefits and challenges. A uniquely Elven aesthetic was already well established, but it was also important that these Elves stand apart from those seen before,

with their own signature shapes, colours and styles. The film also saw the return of Legolas and Tauriel, and Thranduil's emergence in battle armour, giving the audience a glimpse of a true Elf Lord revealed in full wrath and violent glory.

ELVEN SOLDIERS

Before the character of Tauriel was fully defined there was the notion of a female huntress. We began conceptualizing her alongside the Elven armour. The two design paths overlapped and intertwined, influencing each other as we went along because it was assumed that either she or other female Elves would appear in the battle at the climax of the trilogy.

Daniel Falconer, Weta Workshop Designer

Birds feature prominently throughout *The Hobbit* with eagles, the thrush, ravens, Radagast's birds and others. A raven feather motif was something we looked at for our female Elf character, which cued into the leafmaille shapes we ended up pursuing for the soldiers, male and female. There was a strong Japanese influence in our design direction with the Elves at the time. We were looking at things like Hakama pants and using a lot of silk. The feather-maille was looking like it could be an oily, gloss black, which would contrast with areas of bright metallic shine or an accent colour.

Paul Tobin, Weta Workshop Designer

Our colour palette for the soldiers started out in cold blues, a winter colour theme, but as we went along the gold and green came to dominate. The shapes we were exploring for helmets and armour had their origins in what had been done for *The Lord of the Rings*, though we all liked the idea of these broad, fan-shaped crests on the helmets which would be a new element to help set the Mirkwood Elves apart.

Paul Tobin, Weta Workshop Designer

Our starting point for the final incarnation of the Elven soldiers was the palace guard armour designed for Thranduil's guards (*above*), seen in the second film. The lead for that suit of armour with the fan-shaped helmet had been established early, so that became our jumping-off point as we embarked on a new round of armour design. The Elven rider I initially painted (*right*) was essentially the palace guard with the face veil removed.

Nick Keller, Weta Workshop Designer

The fan shape of the helmet crest became a very strong element in the design, becoming quite dramatic in the final version. We had officers' and standard soldiers' versions as well, which included some variation in colour.

Nick Keller, Weta Workshop Designer

NK
WW

NK
WW

NK
WW

PT
WW

NK
WW

PT
WW

PT
WW

Many of the Elven shields were conceived by imagining shields from Mycenaean or even Pelasgian Greece, and revisiting them with Celtic curves and lines. Often, the cross-media transposition of design and motif can offer up surprising results. Imagine the essence of pottery designs and applying that to weapons – unexpected proportions and unusual symmetry of line are often the welcome result.

John Howe, Concept Art Director

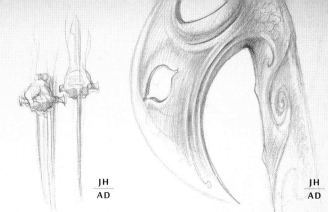

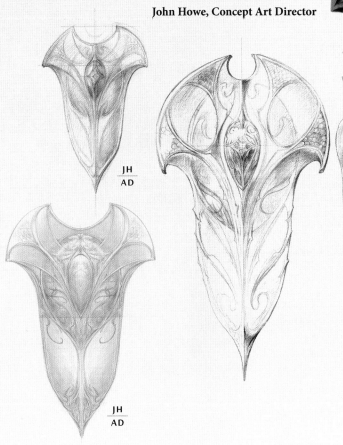

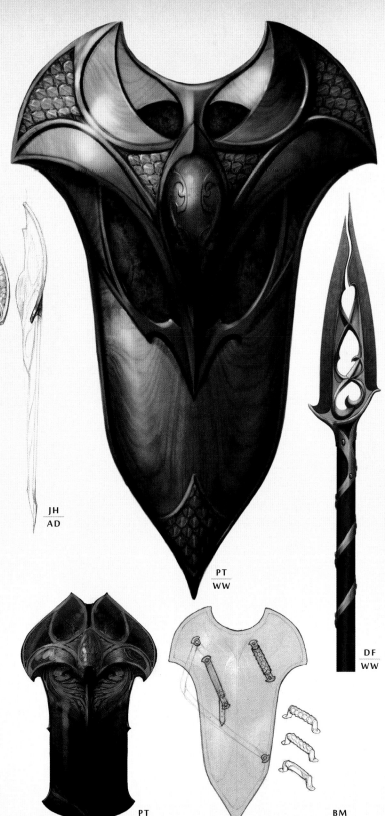

I always liked the idea of polished wood being a feature of the Mirkwood Elven weapons and armour. I had suggested some dark, lacquered wooden handles for the weaponry in my early work. While they didn't get used we did get some beautiful stained and polished wood grain in there, most notably in the shield.

John had drawn a very beautiful shield which Ben Mauro did some additional development work on, including designing a back for it. I worked over the design with some colours and textures, combining wood grain and pine cone-like scales. It was a true combo effort, though the soul of the design was unquestionably John's original drawing. As one of the first things designed and built for the Elves it set the style and influenced the development of their armour.

Paul Tobin, Weta Workshop Designer

I was delighted with how the Elven weaponry and shields evolved on this project, the product of a great working relationship between Weta Workshop's designers and our good friend John Howe, who tackled the assignment in close collaboration. Very quickly a portfolio of exquisite design was generated, achieving a familiar and yet fresh aesthetic that was unquestionably Elven without repeating what we had seen from Rivendell or Lothlórien.

And thanks to the quality of the work Peter was quick to approve a number of key pieces early on in the project. This head start allowed us time to execute the designs as three-dimensional objects with the great care and attention we needed in order to convey the depth of craftsmanship and handmade quality the audience has come to equate with and expect from Elves.

Ultimately much of that responsibility fell upon Paintshop Supervisor Sourisak Chanpaseuth and the Paint Department team here at Weta Workshop. Long-time devotees of Peter's films may remember Sourisak and fellow painter Johnny Brough from *The Lord of the Rings* days, when they were both part of our design team. Their work can be found in the art books that covered those days and their influence seen in some of the armour and weapons that we conceived for those films. By the time of *The Hobbit* Sourisak and Johnny, along with Prosthetics Painting Team Leader Dordi Moen, had established themselves as the core of our painting team, so it fell on their shoulders to translate the complex lacquered wood grains, inlays and metallic effects of the concept art into reality. I couldn't be more proud of the effects they achieved. The Mirkwood Elf weaponry, including swords, daggers, scabbards, pole arms, quivers, arrows, bows, and the beautiful shield, were all splendid props worthy of display in a museum. It almost seemed a shame to send them into battle!

Richard Taylor,
Weta Workshop Design & Special Effects Supervisor

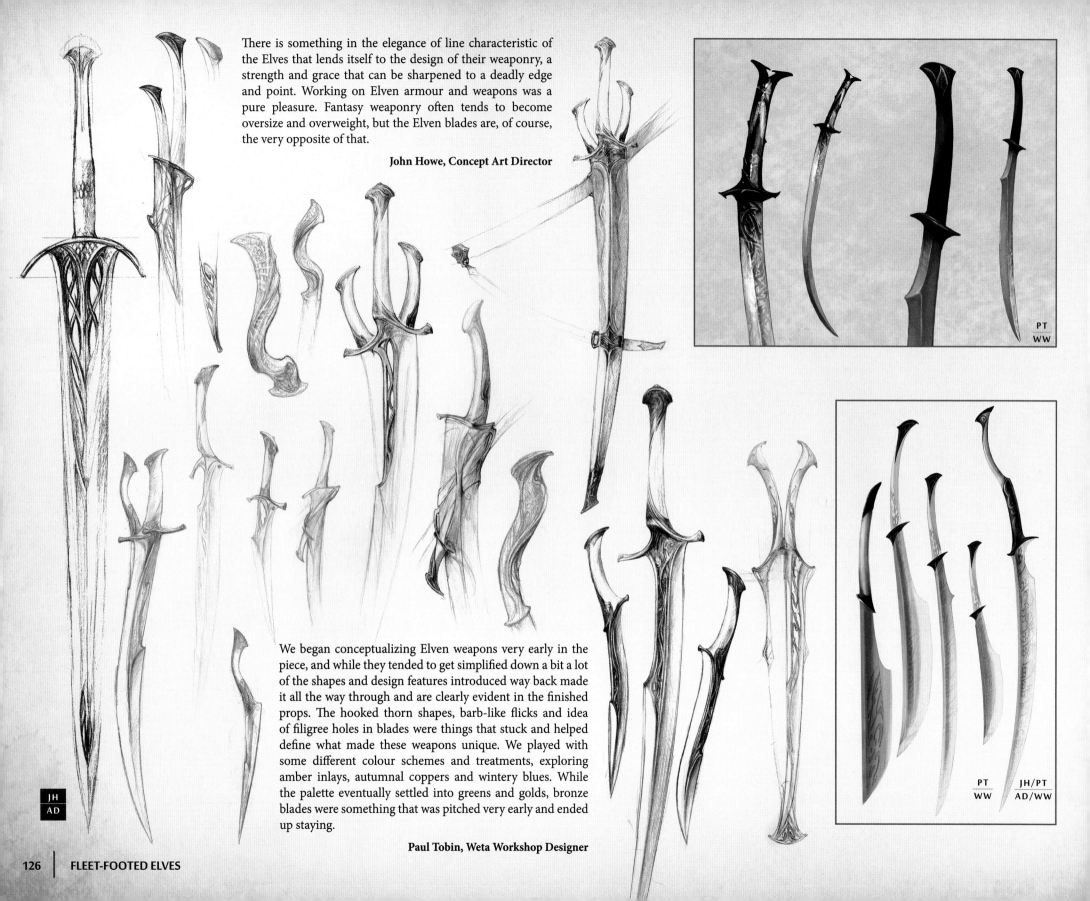

There is something in the elegance of line characteristic of the Elves that lends itself to the design of their weaponry, a strength and grace that can be sharpened to a deadly edge and point. Working on Elven armour and weapons was a pure pleasure. Fantasy weaponry often tends to become oversize and overweight, but the Elven blades are, of course, the very opposite of that.

John Howe, Concept Art Director

We began conceptualizing Elven weapons very early in the piece, and while they tended to get simplified down a bit a lot of the shapes and design features introduced way back made it all the way through and are clearly evident in the finished props. The hooked thorn shapes, barb-like flicks and idea of filigree holes in blades were things that stuck and helped define what made these weapons unique. We played with some different colour schemes and treatments, exploring amber inlays, autumnal coppers and wintery blues. While the palette eventually settled into greens and golds, bronze blades were something that was pitched very early and ended up staying.

Paul Tobin, Weta Workshop Designer

Our Elf weapon exploration started by looking at Eastern blade shapes, weapons like the Japanese katana, but as we went along the influence became more Middle-eastern – single-edged, curved and with dangerous-looking flicks.

One of the big breakthroughs we had was a beautiful dagger that John Howe designed with holes cut in the blade between interlacing thorn and leaf shapes. It was so unique that I leaped on it and tried to reinforce the idea as a feature in my weapon concepts from that point onwards.

Paul Tobin, Weta Workshop Designer

We made much use of cut-outs, both to lighten the weapons and to define their silhouettes. I was particularly fond of the double-ended halberds that I hoped the Elven troops might carry. Testing, though, in the parking lot at Stone Street, proved that they needed a good deal of room to be used safely – hardly available in the mad melée of the battle.

John Howe, Concept Art Director

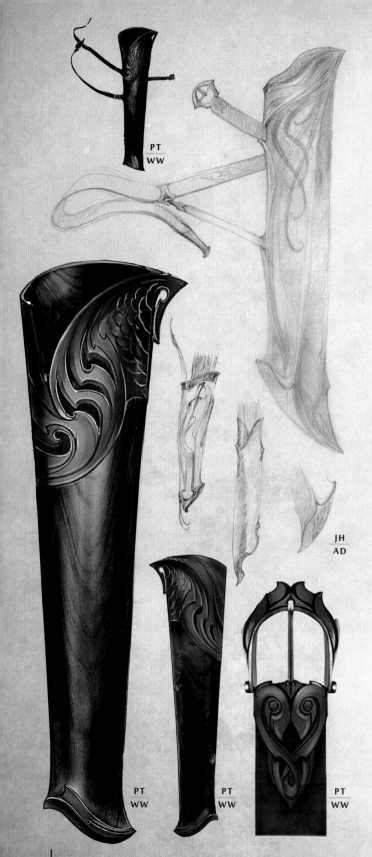

PT
WW

JH
AD

PT
WW

PT
WW

PT
WW

BB
CD

ELVEN SCOUTS

We had seen the mottled and textured camouflage of the hunters and the formal armour of the palace guards in *The Desolation of Smaug*, but our first new Elven costumes in *The Battle of the Five Armies* were the Silvan travelling wear. As we saw Tauriel wearing when she left the forest to follow the Dwarves in the second film, the Silvan Elves have a light outfit that they wear when travelling beyond the confines of Mirkwood. These costumes were suede and silk with a matt, organic quality, and styled with both Tauriel's green ranging outfit and Arwen's riding costume from *The Lord of the Rings* in mind. They moved quite beautifully.

We kept the colours autumnal and the imagery derived from barbed vines and creeping organic matter of the kind with which Mirkwood was filled. We were conscious of the class system that exists in Mirkwood Elf society. Thranduil and his family keep themselves distinct from the rank and file Silvan Elves who make up his populace and of which Tauriel is one. I thought of Thranduil's elite guard as perhaps being in his tier, but the less armoured, lightly clad Elves such as these were Silvan. I imagined they would be agile and rely on their speed and stealth rather than armour. They were more like a Special Forces unit, moving quickly and unseen, so lighter clothing was essential.

Bob Buck, Costume Designer

LEGOLAS
COSTUME & ARMOUR

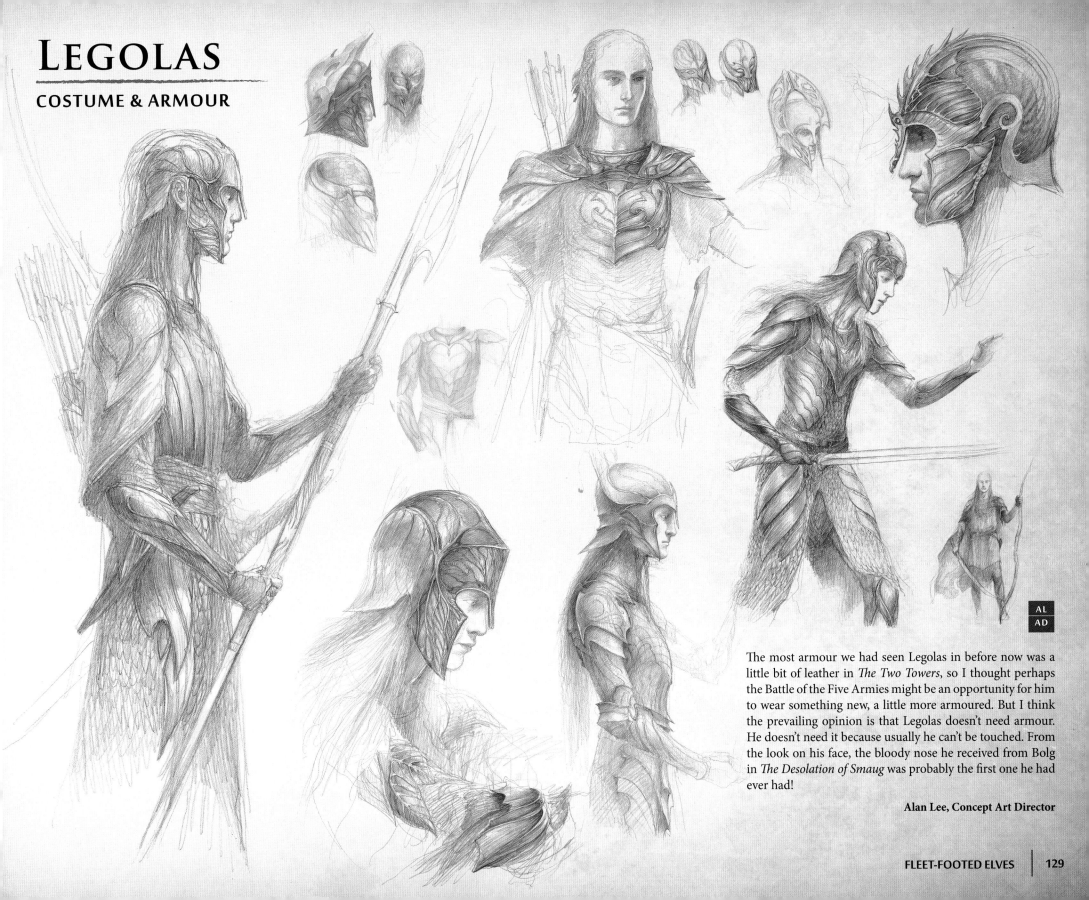

The most armour we had seen Legolas in before now was a little bit of leather in *The Two Towers*, so I thought perhaps the Battle of the Five Armies might be an opportunity for him to wear something new, a little more armoured. But I think the prevailing opinion is that Legolas doesn't need armour. He doesn't need it because usually he can't be touched. From the look on his face, the bloody nose he received from Bolg in *The Desolation of Smaug* was probably the first one he had ever had!

Alan Lee, Concept Art Director

Since we never saw Legolas in armour in *The Lord of the Rings* (with the exception of the Rohan shoulder guards he picked up at Helm's Deep) I wondered if he might not don a full suit for the Battle of the Five Armies. As with the other Elven armour, I hoped that the motifs could in a sense ignore the pieced structure of the armour, flowing seamlessly from one overlapping plate to the next. It would have been fascinating to explore thinner materials, to give Legolas a truly form-hugging full armour, and depart from the traditional steel.

John Howe, Concept Art Director

LEGOLAS

WEAPONS

Legolas had been using the bow, arrows, quiver and white knives (*second from right*) he carried in *The Lord of the Rings*, but once Thranduil got his cool sword I think everyone felt a bit sorry for old Leggy! It was time he got a new weapon so we set about designing a larger sword for him. My idea was to make a two-handed sword version of his knives (*right*), which we actually had approved and made, but then the idea was suggested that it made a lot of sense for him to commandeer Orcrist from Thorin, so that's ended up in the film.

Daniel Falconer, Weta Workshop Designer

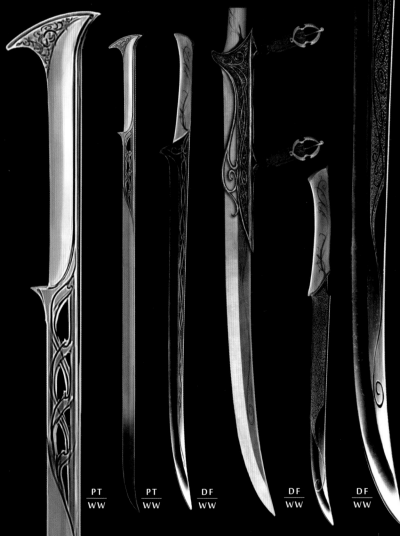

PT / WW   PT / WW   DF / WW   DF / WW   DF / WW

THRANDUIL

Like our early explorations for the Mirkwood soldier armour, Thranduil's early armour studies bore strong Eastern influences with lots of lacquered black wood, inlays of accent colours and even the idea of an impassive, sculptural half-mask that would slide down over his face in battle. I thought of him like a Japanese emperor and gave him a striking headdress/helmet and twin daggers at his hips; the mask would make him seem even more dispassionate and imposing.

Paul Tobin, Weta Workshop Designer

Once the antlers had appeared as one of Thranduil's symbols, it was tempting to put them on his helmet. The style of armour is 5th century, a mix of Scythian and early Roman gladiatorial, with a full skirt and a lamed breastplate. Would it have been practical in battle? If the incredibly extravagant Japanese helms are any hint, possibly.

John Howe, Concept Art Director

For me, the creation of Thranduil's armour and weapons was one of the highlights of working on *The Hobbit* films. The armour design was something a number of our team tackled, working closely with Costume Designer Bob Buck. Ultimately Daniel Falconer landed it for us with the support of Nick Keller and Paul Tobin. Daniel also designed the sword Thranduil would wield. Peter liked it so much that he decided Actor Lee Pace should have two of them in the final battle! It is one of my favourite blades across all the projects we have worked on at Weta Workshop, with its hollow handgrip and long, perforated blade all cut from a single length of steel. It was a joy to watch Lee swinging it on set with such brutal efficiency and grace.

Richard Taylor,
Weta Workshop Design & Special Effects Supervisor

I had a quick pass at designing a dagger for Thranduil when there was going to be a scene that required it. The concept was essentially to create something in keeping with the sword Daniel Falconer had designed (*far right*), so I preserved the same lines and patterns, but shrunk and simplified the blade (*near right, and in scabbard, near right, bottom*).

Paul Tobin, Weta Workshop Designer

Peter wanted the sight of Thranduil in action to be like a maelstrom. He would be a swirling vortex of death. A way to show this was through the movement of the snow in the air around him, with his flashing blades leaving a trail of swirling snow and blood as he cleaved his way through the battle.

Greg Tozer, Weta Workshop Designer

The way the sequence was described to us, Thranduil was holding back to begin with in the battle for Dale, but once he decides to get involved himself we should see something extraordinary. This is Legolas's father, after all, a Lord among the Sindar Elves.

Thranduil struck me as a character who would move about with the greatest economy and quiet, effortless grace, but when moved to wrath he would be a killing machine. There was always the risk with Legolas and some of his stunts that we would be in superhero territory, and these ideas for Thranduil did skirt dangerously close to that, but at the same time there had to be a 'Aw heck, yeah!' moment when we saw him truly unleash on his foes. With the concepts that I pitched I strived to balance supernatural Elven daring-do and the need for eye-popping action with some believability.

That said, this particular gag idea pushed it pretty far (*left, middle & bottom*): having Thranduil go over the walls of Dale, whirling his way across the face of the masonry. I imagined him alternately wedging his sword-tips, like climbing axes, in the mortar as he took out hulking Orc climbing creatures attempting to ascend the wall. Each creature wore frames on their backs, trailing chains hung with Orc troops that it was dragging with it up the wall, like living siege machinery. A single swipe of his sword and Thranduil could send a beast and his retinue of troops hurtling into the chasm.

The idea didn't stick, but I could see it playing cinematically in my mind's eye.

Daniel Falconer, Weta Workshop Designer

Of course, with an antlered throne and livery, it made sense that Thranduil would ride an elk. I always very much enjoy changing the silhouette of animals, in this case giving the elk a horse's more muscular and arched neck and more elegant flanks. For the horns, it was eventually the Irish Elk, or more correctly the *Megatherium*, that carried the day. The saddle is high, like a medieval saddle, with the rider sitting well off the mount's back.

John Howe, Concept Art Director

JH
AD

AL
WD

JH
AD

JH
AD

JH
AD

JH
AD

MH
AD

MH
AD

MH
AD

Grim Dwarves in Shining Maille

Dwarves of Erebor & the Iron Hills

The reclamation of Erebor sees Thorin and his Company of Dwarves proudly readopting the trappings and mantles of their heritage. Dressed in Dwarven finery and armed with Dwarf-made weapons, they set about ordering and defending their home and its great riches, for it is not long before Thorin's claim to the treasure of Smaug is challenged.

From the Iron Hills in the east come reinforcements, as Dain leads his host of grim soldiers over the saddle of the Mountain's south-east arm and into position between Erebor and the allied Lake-town and Mirkwood crowds occupying Dale. When war comes Thorin and his followers emerge from behind their walls to charge into battle clad in gleaming armour, swinging axes, swords, flails and hammers as they cut through Azog's army.

The chance to depict Dwarves as Dwarves again, clad in raiment and plate complementing their stature and nature was an opportunity relished by Nick Keller, Designer at Weta Workshop, who quickly established himself as the Dwarf armour go-to guy. Alongside his other design responsibilities and over the course of several years, Nick steadily waded through the long list of Dwarf armour needing to be conceptualized, including Iron Hill soldiers, Dain and regal armoured versions of the thirteen members of the Company of Thorin. Nick also worked closely with Costume Designer Bob Buck, who was responsible for creating Erebor reclaimed and battle costumes for the leads.

Weta Workshop's construction swan song on the trilogy came in the form of a huge practical war chariot prop to be ridden by Thorin and his nephews as they ploughed a channel through the battle to a fateful confrontation with Azog and his warriors.

IRON HILL DWARF ARMOUR

DF
WW

The armour worn by the Dwarves we saw in Erebor and then later in battle outside Moria in *An Unexpected Journey* (*top, near right*) was originally designed to be for the Iron Hill Dwarves. When it was allocated to the Erebor Dwarves it meant we were starting from scratch again with a new army to develop.

The boar motif was established early on as an icon of this particular army, based on the idea that their cavalry might ride boars. Later that became something particular to Dain, but a stylized boar motif was one of the driving elements as we began exploring the Iron Hill armour.

Nick Keller, Weta Workshop Designer

NK
WW

NK
WW

NK
WW

We explored a few different looks based on various real-world cultural references. There was some Nordic influence that crept in. In the early concepts the faceplates especially were Viking-esque. Peter reacted well to the general shape of a rounded armour design I came up with (*top right, second from right*), but asked for a reinterpretation that had more faceting, replacing the curved armour plates with faceted surfaces (*top right*). As I began working on the helmet I thought of the facets as being analogous to the faces of a cut gem stone. It was a statement about the precision of the Dwarven craftsmen and their ability to manipulate metals with extraordinary skill, producing working, articulated armour that was devoid of curves.

Nick Keller, Weta Workshop Designer

NK
WW

ST
WW

ST
WW

I created a number of helmet variants with the idea being that there would be ranks within the army that could be identified by their helmets, starting with the very simple ones of the basic soldiers, the more elaborate officers and then finally Dain's own helmet, which had the largest crest.

Nick Keller, Weta Workshop Designer

The question of colour took a while to answer. Initially we started quite cool, with a steel-blue and grey look, very wintery. The colours were in flux because we were designing the other armies simultaneously. It was always in the back of our minds that in the midst of quick cuts and lots of action, or sweeping shots high above the battlefield, it was important that the various armies be chromatically distinct so people could tell what was going on.

We were manufacturing armour components before we had the colour completely nailed down and the Weta Workshop Paint Department, run by Sourisak Chanpaseuth, produced some really interesting colour passes with unusual mottling and iridescent variations that had an almost oily look to them. Then with the final layer of ageing and wear and tear applied the results were very interesting. We had looked at a coppery colouration for certain parts of the armour but those elements ended up becoming more yellow-gold, juxtaposed over a bluish-purple steel.

Nick Keller, Weta Workshop Designer

Iron Hill Dwarf Weapons & Props

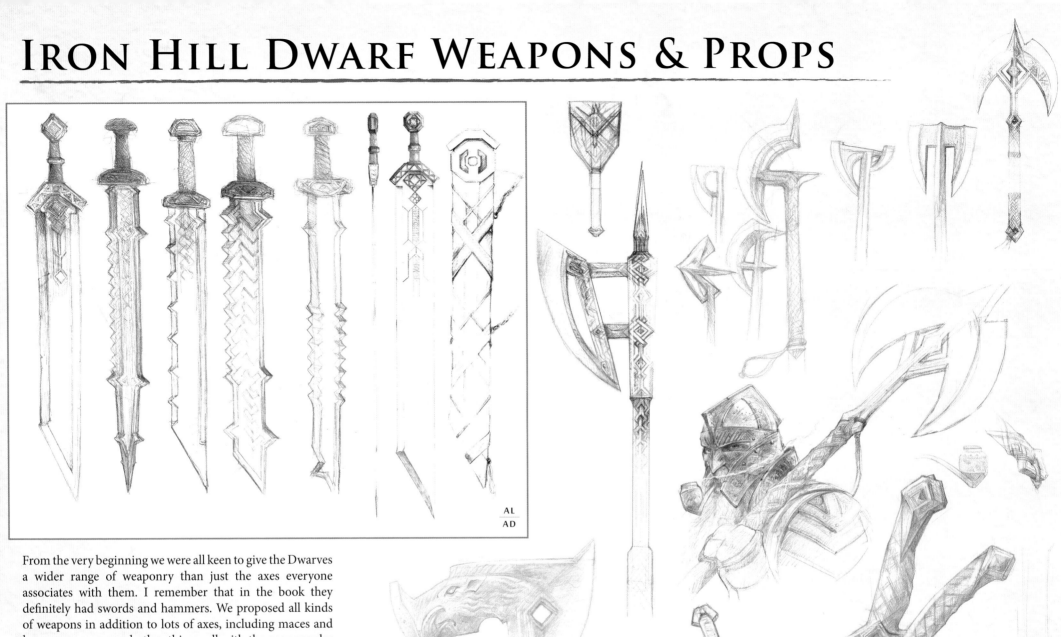

From the very beginning we were all keen to give the Dwarves a wider range of weaponry than just the axes everyone associates with them. I remember that in the book they definitely had swords and hammers. We proposed all kinds of weapons in addition to lots of axes, including maces and hammers, spears and other things, all with the very angular Dwarf aesthetic that had been clearly established already.

Nick Keller, Weta Workshop Designer

I drew many Dwarven axes, first for Thorin and Co., and later for the Iron Hill army. The spike at the bottom of the blade (*facing page, upper left pencil drawings*) mirrors the tusks of the armoured boars they ride into battle.

John Howe, Concept Art Director

AL
AD

JH
AD

JH
AD

SL
WW

NK
WW

NK
WW

NK
WW

NK
WW

NK
WW

NK
WW

NK
WW

ST
WW

ST
WW

NK
WW

NK
WW

One of the more 'out there' ideas that came up in the designs was something Peter brought up for us to explore, as he was curious to see how it might look. The idea was that there was a kind of projectile that would be positioned on a base-plate, which the Dwarf would stomp on to flick up into the air and then swat like a baseball player with the back of his axe to fire into the enemy ranks (*above*). As goofy as it might sound, it was an idea that was worth exploring because it gave the Dwarves a very unique weapon and way of fighting that could be very memorable.

Nick Keller, Weta Workshop Designer

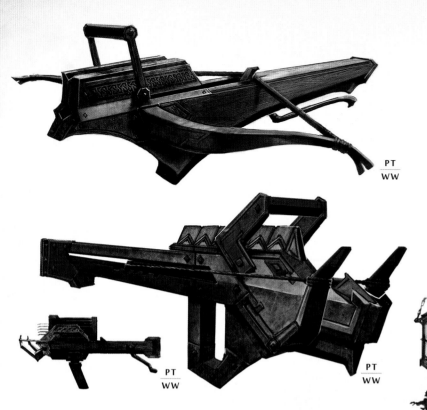

We always thought of the Dwarves as being crossbowmen rather than bowmen, but the problem with crossbows is that they can be quite complicated things. Dwarves are master craftsmen and mechanically-minded problem-solvers, so the idea of a specialized crossbow that perhaps even had a repeating action, which would be more cinematic than a traditional crossbow reload, didn't seem implausible. What was really cool was when Peter brought in a 14th century crossbow from his personal collection and left it on the couch in our design room library for us to look at and study. I started playing with how a Dwarf crossbow might look and hit on the notion of using the raven motif in some way. The back end of the design I proposed for our 'crow-bow' was firmly rooted in the historic bow, but I turned the front end into something that looked more Dwarven.

Paul Tobin, Weta Workshop Designer

During *The Lord of the Rings* we visited and explored many different Middle-earth cultures, but even though we spent significant time in Moria it was an abandoned city, so we never really got much of a chance to develop or explore the culture of the Dwarves. Gimli was our one example of a Dwarf with much screen time, but he was a single character away from home. With *The Hobbit* we had the chance to go nuts with the Dwarves. It was enormous fun developing the Iron Hill Dwarf army, imagining and building their armour, weapons, fighting techniques and racial personality. The army we created for the films had its roots in Tolkien's writings, but there was also lots of room for us to embellish it and create icons that would set the Dwarves apart from Elves, men and Orcs. The Iron Hill army brought with it formidable armaments and brutal weaponry, with chariots drawn by giant, armoured goats and a leader borne into battle astride a ferocious boar! It was one of the rare and special legacy-building design briefs that come along only occasionally, to develop a credible and hopefully memorable aesthetic for a relatively untouched culture that is so important in fantasy mythology.

**Richard Taylor,
Weta Workshop Design & Special Effects Supervisor**

As we went along it turned out that Peter wanted a crossbow that wasn't a crossbow – something which might have a similar basic launching mechanism but fired in a way that looked a bit different, so the Dwarf crossbowmen would have their own distinct visual style. The solution came in the way the string pulled on the arms, which ended up being a boar's tusks, pulling downwards instead of outwards and back.

Nick Keller, Weta Workshop Designer

With the pig theme coming through so strong we dubbed the new Dwarf crossbow the 'boar-lista'. Peter liked our solution to the firing mechanism but still felt the wooden stock was too bulky, so we stripped that out and replaced it with metal, punching holes in it to save weight. Ed Denton in our 3D Modelling Department did a lot of the problem-solving work on it.

Paul Tobin, Weta Workshop Designer

There was the idea of a Dwarven piper being part of the battle. I thought that was a cool idea and threw in a drawing that I did under Dan Hennah's direction. John Howe had an alternative take on the idea (*page 8*). We each championed our concept, as you do, and pushed them as hard as we could. For a while it looked like mine was going to win but I think John's did in the end.

The process of making these movies is both collaborative and competitive, and it's great fun because of both those things. I can honestly say that in every instance, the more layered a concept became with different people's ideas added and battled over, the better the results tended to be. In the end an idea is an idea, and it gets used or it doesn't, or it evolves into something stronger, but you don't get attached to an idea. You push it as far as it can go and then move on to the next challenge.

Anthony Allan, Concept Artist

DAIN IRONFOOT

Discussing Dain, Nick Keller and I concluded that we wanted his armour to be the most beautifully complex of all the Dwarf suits that we were making. Given who the character was, his costume demanded a level of surface treatment and detail that would represent the Dwarves at their most skilled, but this complexity couldn't override the importance of first establishing a strong, iconic form. We were looking for a statement that was stout and compact, like a humanoid tank, but beautiful, proud and regal as well as dangerous, all at once.

Richard Taylor,
Weta Workshop Design & Special Effects Supervisor

Dain's armoured look grew out of the Iron Hill Dwarf armour we were designing, although his was more elaborate and complex. We ended up dialling back the complexity a bit and using the basic Iron Hill soldier as a base, making a more ornate version for their leader. The boar was always part of the Iron Hill aesthetic, but as this evolved it became Dain's main motif.

Nick Keller, Weta Workshop Designer

143

The concept as I introduced it was far too cartoonish, but I can lay some claim to the genesis of the tusked beard idea for Dain that later became a signature for his character. There had been so many Dwarves in the films up to this point so introducing a new one called for something memorable and unique that would set him apart. Peter asked us to offer up bold ideas for new directions so I threw in a hastily painted concept of a crazy beard that was twisted into two huge decorative tusks like those on a pig (*left, middle*). As Peter pointed out, it went too far, but he liked the idea of them along with the razorback boar-like hackles in his hair, evoking a Mohawk, so we looked at ways we could include them in a less over-the-top fashion.

Paul Tobin, Weta Workshop Designer

We talked a lot about who Dain was and how we might make him distinct from the members of Thorin's Company. The direction we took was making him look feral but also grandiose, the pinnacle of a Dwarven badass, wild and windswept. I didn't think of him as a vain character, so his decorative elements would be a necessary acknowledgement of his authority, the trappings of rank that he was expected to wear and not just self-adornment.

Some months later we had a second round of design on Dain when Peter asked us to conceive him without the restrictions of costume and make-up. What had been achieved on Actor Billy Connolly with the prosthetic make-up and costume was cool, but it hadn't given Peter, Fran and Philippa exactly what they wanted from the character and we all felt that Billy had become a bit lost under it all. Paradoxically, if Dain were entirely digital we could bring more of Billy to the front and have his expressions read more clearly, so that became the new design brief. At the same time we could shift his proportions in subtle ways that costume could only achieve to a certain degree. We were able to broaden him, enlarge his head in relation to his body and make him feel chunkier, without encumbering Billy's performance the way a heavy costume, armour and prosthetics had (*facing page, inset, bottom right*).

Greg Tozer, Weta Workshop Designer

I welcomed the chance to have another go at Dain's look. I loved what had been achieved but felt like we had thrown everything except the kitchen sink at him. I flattened his skull and stripped away some of the scarring, hair and tattoos to open his face, hopefully allowing Billy's natural expressiveness to shine through again.

Daniel Falconer, Weta Workshop Designer

DF
WW

AL
AD

GT
WW

GT
WW

GT
WW

NK
WW

We had begun designing axes for Thrain when it was mentioned that in the literature Tolkien refers to him having a red axe. It's not clear exactly what he was referring to when he calls it red, whether it is just bloody or whether it is actually red in colour, but we took it as being literally red as it gave us an opportunity to come up with a very cool, signature weapon for him. We had made an axe of jade for Dwalin, so with that in mind it was suggested that perhaps Dain's weapon might be carved out of a kind of stone that was blood red in colour and could handle being wielded in battle without shattering. Initially we had been thinking of it as a metal axe that had been lacquered or enamelled for decorative reasons, but when it came down to it, the choice was made to create the prop to look like crimson stone.

Nothing was wasted. Earlier axe designs for Dain that weren't used but had been prototyped ended up being recycled as axes for the Dwarves fighting outside Moria.

Nick Keller, Weta Workshop Designer

Playing off his beard colour and the idea of his red axe, I put a lot of red in the leather and garment components of Dain's armour to help him stand out. We also ended up making the crest of his helmet red. The helmet went through many variations with different crest designs, but the core of the idea was the bristling back of a razorback pig. I liked the idea that it was so large on him that it gave the Dwarf some extra height.

Nick Keller, Weta Workshop Designer

ED
WW

NK
WW

The wonderful Billy Connolly played Dain, Lord of the Iron Hills and eventual King of the Dwarves of Durin. We made a costume for Dain's coronation consisting of regal purple robes, richly embroidered with gold on the cuffs, recalling Thror's coat and that which Thorin adopted upon reclaiming the Mountain.

Bob Buck, Costume Designer

We worked closely with the Costume Department on all the Dwarves including Dain, so I offered a suggestion for what his coronation robes might look like, pulling the red from his armour and axe as his main colour. It was a strong colour that I imagined would stand out.

Nick Keller, Weta Workshop Designer

DWARF WAR MOUNTS

I was enjoying myself putting Dwarves on different animals for the battle: a bison, ibex, boar, a bull... I had our Assistant Coordinator Jack Tippler pose for me on a chair and took some reference pictures. He was getting into the motions for me and almost fell off just as I snapped a photo, which ended up being perfect!

Anthony Allan, Concept Artist

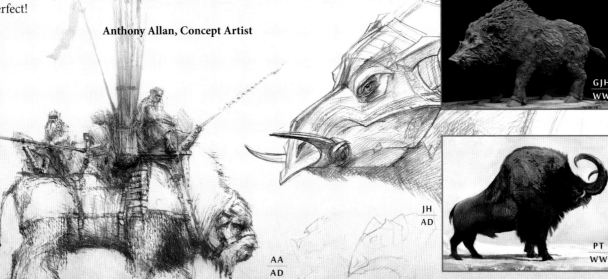

In thinking about a Dwarf's characteristics and trying to marry them with a mount that might share those traits, I kept coming back to a boar. It just seemed like a fantastic fit and the thought of armoured boars charging around the battlefield was too much fun not to pitch. I stayed at work late one night and painted up a concept, well into the small hours. To my great delight, when it was presented the next day the idea gained traction and before long we were developing concepts around pig-riding Dwarves.

In my original idea the Dwarf cavalry rode conventional European wild boar, but in the course of the design process the team explored new varieties of swine, some borrowing features from African warthogs and some with truly outrageous tusks. Peter was never one to settle for the conventional!

Daniel Falconer, Weta Workshop Designer

A lot of art had been produced depicting the riding beasts in heavy armour, but Production Designer Dan Hennah's thinking was that the Dwarf boars didn't necessarily have to be heavily armoured. If they were unarmoured they could be lighter and faster, and boars are practically bullet-proof anyhow (*above*).

Anthony Allan, Concept Artist

We experimented with all kinds of pigs for the Dwarves. The main variation that we went back and forth on was whether or not they would be more akin to a warthog with huge tusks or based on a kunekune pig with its fat, squashed-in face. There are some amazing looking pig-like creatures when you look back into our fossil history, some with hippopotamus-like features and huge mouths, which I thought would be terrifying to see on the battlefield, so I drew upon those for some of my designs. One thing Peter always liked was the bristly manes running down their backs. Towards the end he began to favour the kunekune look (*below*), but then it was also decided that the boar would be something particular to Dain himself.

Nick Keller, Weta Workshop Designer

Once it was decided that the rest of the Dwarves would ride or be pulled by sheep or goats, I tried to get the shapes in the armour worn by Dain's boar to complement those of his own armour. It created something quite special, having him as the lone boar-rider, so I took my shape cues from the shoulder armour of Dain's plates and put him on a high saddle based on a profile picture John Howe had done; I then harmonized the articulated metal into something that I hoped would work well in motion with him astride it.

Nick Keller, Weta Workshop Designer

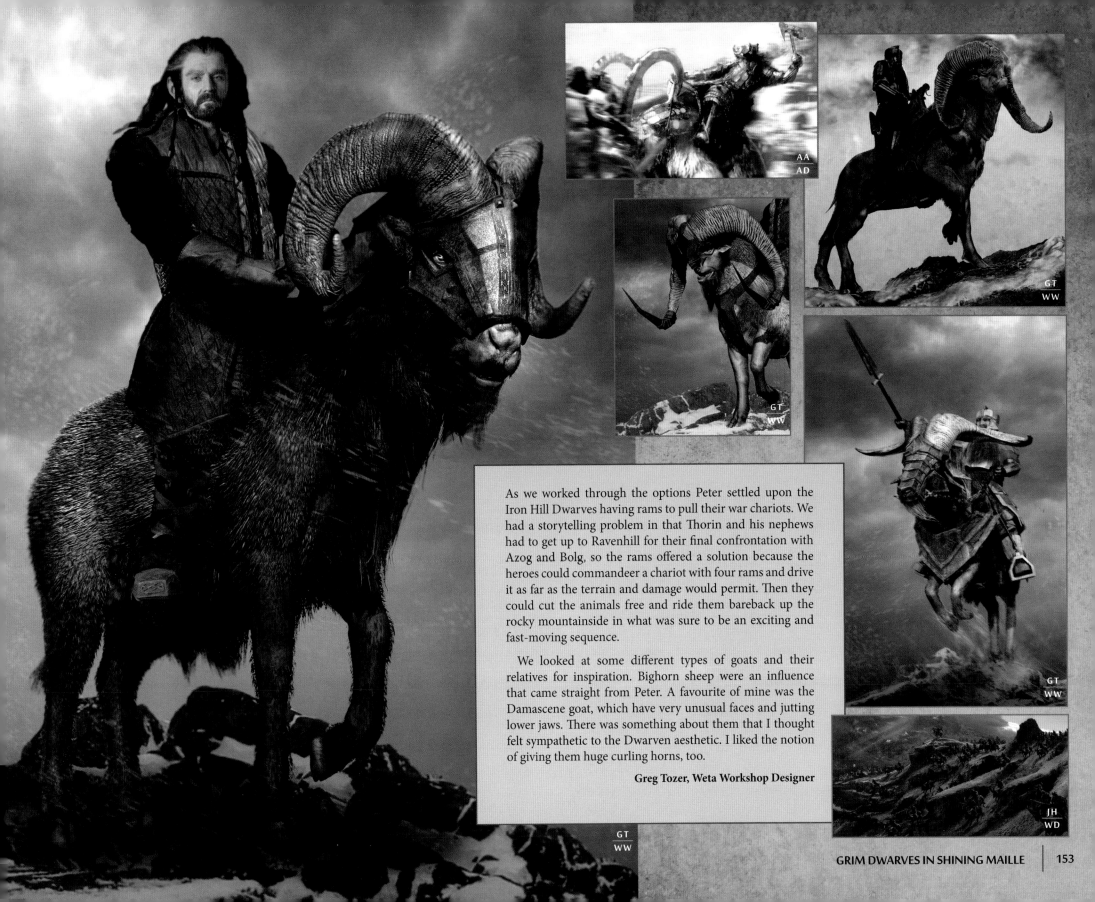

As we worked through the options Peter settled upon the Iron Hill Dwarves having rams to pull their war chariots. We had a storytelling problem in that Thorin and his nephews had to get up to Ravenhill for their final confrontation with Azog and Bolg, so the rams offered a solution because the heroes could commandeer a chariot with four rams and drive it as far as the terrain and damage would permit. Then they could cut the animals free and ride them bareback up the rocky mountainside in what was sure to be an exciting and fast-moving sequence.

We looked at some different types of goats and their relatives for inspiration. Bighorn sheep were an influence that came straight from Peter. A favourite of mine was the Damascene goat, which have very unusual faces and jutting lower jaws. There was something about them that I thought felt sympathetic to the Dwarven aesthetic. I liked the notion of giving them huge curling horns, too.

Greg Tozer, Weta Workshop Designer

DWARF WAR CHARIOT

Early in the project I had an idea for a Dwarven war chariot. I thought it could be used at the battle, perhaps by Dain. It would be pulled by prehistoric goats and run straight into the melee in an echo of ancient battles, akin to Roman or Egyptian chariots charging against infantry. I really liked the idea of these white furry goats on a snowy landscape.

Frank Victoria, Weta Workshop Designer

The idea of a Dwarf war chariot started out as a way to give Dain a grand entrance. We started out with some quite classical chariot shapes, but it became a heavier and heavier vehicle as we went along. Peter was keen on it being well-armoured and angular, with vicious blades so that it could mow through enemies. At one point we even had a trailer on it.

As the script developed the chariot became something that Thorin and his group would use to cut a way through to Ravenhill, where Azog was, and Peter liked the idea of a big crossbow weapon being mounted on it for that sequence. That dictated the design to a certain degree as we played with where the driver would be in relation to the gunner or gunners. In some designs we had two crossbows, but in the final version the driver, who was to be Thorin, was behind and above the gunner.

Nick Keller, Weta Workshop Designer

The big chariot-mounted crossbow had a V-shaped crossbow bolt feed, mostly because it looked cool and different. One of the best things about the chariot and its weapon was that we got to make it as a huge, life-size, working prop.

Nick Keller, Weta Workshop Designer

NK/GT
———
WW

NK
———
WW

NK
———
WW

I am a physical effects guy at heart. As much as it is gratifying to design something that is then rendered digitally to such an accomplished degree, I love making things with my hands, so it was a true pleasure to round out the work that we did on *The Hobbit* trilogy with a huge physical build. Frank Victoria, Nick Keller and the team had been developing a fantastic war chariot for the Dwarves to ride into battle. Peter settled on a design and then turned it over to our team of practical effects artists to build life-size as a working prop. I remember when we were adding the finishing touches to it our crew all coming down to the studio to pose with this huge war machine. There was a great feeling of accomplishment, not just for what we had just made, but also to be able to round out our time in Middle-earth with such a satisfying and awe-inspiring physical build.

Richard Taylor,
Weta Workshop Design & Special Effects Supervisor

GT
———
WW

RECLAIMED EREBOR DWARF COSTUMES

Once Smaug has left the building the Dwarves begin to feel comfortable again and quickly settle back into what was once their home. They are only too pleased to cast off their borrowed Lake-town clothes and dress like Dwarves again, finding clothing in rooms, cupboards, closets and the armoury of Erebor. It's a celebration of their reclamation, of being Dwarves again, of regaining their identities.

We took them back to the colours established in the first film with their travelling costumes, which were inspired by the hood colours Tolkien gave them. Their new garments had to be rich and proud, but also a little bit degraded from having been hanging in closets for so long.

Essentially, we took them back to their undergarments and then threw on one or two new layers, but kept them open and loose, suggesting that the Dwarves were a little more relaxed now that they were back in their own environment. It was part of Peter's brief to us as well – get them looking blocky and Dwarven again as they embrace their Dwarven heritage, but not too buttoned up and stiff. They're less concerned with being all done up and perfect, perhaps with the exception of Dori, who fusses about that sort of thing.

I looked at the shapes in their original travelling garments: a lot of work went in to making those iconic to each character, so we sought to maintain those icons in their Erebor costumes, including reintroducing those colours. We felt we could afford to make the colours quite rich too, given the Dwarves were now back in the richest place in the world. Practically, we had also seen how the 3D cameras tended to suck colour out, so we were compensating for that loss as well.

We looked at embroideries that had a masculine quality to them, perhaps with metallic threads and blocky patterns. Where possible we included metal elements in the costumes, which helped suggest a certain level of craftsmanship and sophistication that we wanted to associate with Erebor as it was before the Dragon. It was a lot of fun pulling out all the processes we had developed and used in the course of the films and putting so many of them to use, along with a bunch of new ones, on these rich costumes.

Bob Buck, Costume Designer

Thorin was descending into a dark place and we wanted to acknowledge and reflect this in his costume. He had become infected with the Dragon curse, the gold sickness. Taking the costume into black personified Thorin's mounting inner turmoil.

We gave him a dark leather tunic with an almost modern street sensibility to it, on top of which Thorin wore a regal coat, presumably his grandfather Thror's. In so doing he has assumed the mantle of kingship, quite literally. The theme of Thorin's entire costume was a mixture of rough and royal, and the coat and rings he wore on his fingers put the final level of royal over the rough.

Bob Buck, Costume Designer

BB
CD

Designing Fili's costume was a little trickier than conceiving some of the other Dwarves' reclaimed Erebor outfits had been. His signature travelling costume colour had been a grey, so we chose to add a little more strength to his new costume by including some more colour. The discussion in the beginning was around making him more purple, perhaps a purplish Air Force blue, the colour of a young prince perhaps? The colour then shifted around a bit. Fili's regal armour had already been designed and approved, so we had to make sure whatever we did would work with that.

Fili was among the Dwarves whom we also cheated slightly, removing bulk from his body suit, which all the Dwarf cast wore under their costumes. They had worn these throughout the films to give them Dwarven physiques, but by this time it was well established and the audience had accepted them as Dwarves. We could therefore afford to relax our rules a little and slim them down for the final battle to give them more heroic proportions.

Balin's return to Erebor saw his costume return to the red hues of his travelling coat from the first film. At this point in his life Balin was more gentleman counsellor than warrior. We gave him a rich coat with a removable fur collar that could be set to the side when he needed to don armour. The coat was woven with motifs and elements of metal detail. There was a lordly aspect to Balin's costuming in keeping with his character. We also gloved him, partly for aesthetic reasons and also because Actor Ken Stott was more comfortable in gloves than the enlarged prosthetic silicone hands all the Dwarves wore to distort their proportions.

Dumping his Lake-town hand-me-downs, Dwalin was back in warrior mode again with a costume of leather and chain. We redefined Dwalin's shape again, with a tight-belted waist and broad shoulders. His garment was fairly simple with a straight military cut to it, very practical and affording him plenty of range for movement. In battle the panels of his skirts would flare like blades as he spun about and the belt helped link his armour and soft costume elements very well. This is what Dwalin would wear to go to work, and when Dwalin goes to work it means someone is taking a beating.

The costume also brought back Dwalin's signature green, with Dwarven motifs pressed into the leather as a textural treatment.

Bob Buck, Costume Designer

BB
CD

Beneath their new gear the Dwarves still wore the last vestiges of their travelling clothes, which were mostly just their underwear and footwear by this stage, well-worn, dirty and aged. We tried to keep it so there was a contrast within the costumes with the top layer of riches, so we weren't creating completely new costumes so much as exchanging the outer elements. Beneath this layer were the Dwarves as we had come to know them.

Even in his reclaimed Erebor ensemble, Bifur was still quite grunty, leathery and rough. Those elements still represented who he was, and just as we did when we established the Dwarves at the beginning of the trilogy, we reinforced a sense of a class system within their number, with Thorin and his family at the top and Bifur and his relations representing the working class. Nevertheless, having reclaimed the Mountain and its treasures from the Dragon, we imagined Bifur would have randomly grabbed some flashy trinkets and thrown them on, serving as gaudy vambraces.

Green had always been in Bombur's palette, in smaller elements for the most part, but for Bombur's reclaimed Erebor costume we pushed it to the fore, using a beautiful chartreuse. The green had always worked so well alongside Bombur's auburn hair and beard. By bringing this out in his new costume this accentuated the orange of his hair, producing a wonderful, colourful result. Based on an idea from Fran we created a kind of waistcoat, which worked very well, and a giant cummerbund to wrap around his waist and complete his look, celebrating his fabulous girth.

Oin was one of the oldest of the Dwarves and we have always tended to treat him in a stately manner. He was like the country doctor of a small village, quite grandfatherly and dressed in wool and quilted velvet for the first film. His colour was brown, which is always tricky. There are some beautiful browns but it is easy to become mired in muddy hues so I wanted to beef up his colour a little for his Erebor costume.

Oin also received a big fur collar. Something we had experimented with on Thrain for the flashback scenes in the first film was layering leather over the fur, which broke it up and gave it another level of interest and texture, catching the light differently.

Bob Buck, Costume Designer

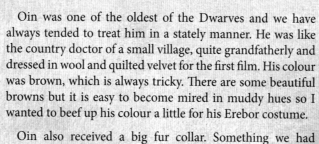

NK
WW

NK/BB
WW/CD

BB
CD

One of the things we did with Ori was to alter his shape for the final battle. Up until now Ori has been portrayed with a high-waisted, soft pot-belly and rounded shoulders. Everything dropped and was soft. To reflect the evolution of his character we shifted his proportions, squishing the belly and making more of his shoulders, giving him some strength and a more traditionally heroic physique.

Creating Nori's Erebor costume was fun. The character has always been described as a bit of a rogue, a poacher, or even a used car salesman. There's a streetwise quality to Jed Brophy's Dwarf that was enjoyable to play to in the costume. Looking at the tunic he wore at the beginning of the trilogy,

we pulled out the collar of his new garment. His new leather tunic was a kind of sleeveless coat with rich printed velvet and a broad collar, snazzy and savvy-looking. With his hair and beard styled back into the iconic prongs with which he started the adventure the collar reinforced those shapes. Peter was a little concerned that the costume was a little bit too seventies in style, but Fran talked him into it. What's wrong with the seventies?

Dori received a lovely coat of red and bluey purples with lots of metal decoration around its wide, shoulder-spanning collar. We embroidered the edges to frame the garment. It's very important to define certain elements of a costume.

Sometimes they can feel unfinished or weak without them. Often we would do this for the centre-front and collar on our Dwarves. We weren't creating cartoon characters, but the eye does like a strong line to land on, so an outline of sorts can be very helpful in establishing key shapes for a character. On *The Hobbit* we also used them to subtly shift and cheat our actors' proportions from human to Dwarf. While the elements were different, such as rich cuffs for his wrists with lots of detail, the overall effect reproduced the silhouette of Dori's first costume from *An Unexpected Journey*.

Bob Buck, Costume Designer

REGAL DWARF ARMOUR & WEAPONS

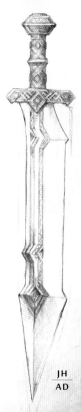

We always knew the regal armour and weapons would be difficult to conceive and create. The bar was set high by Tolkien's description of the Dwarves' resplendent appearance, but in terms of being the climax of our trilogy there was also the demand for the Dwarves emerging in their armour to be a kind of visual highpoint, an 'Oh wow!' moment topping a trilogy's worth of 'wow' moments.

We started early and it quickly became apparent that this was going to be a one-man job when Nick Keller blew us all away with his first exploratory concepts. Nick's artwork was so powerful and his ideas so tight that I knew he had this one covered. Over the course of the half-decade that we were on the project, whenever he wasn't designing something else Nick was diligently plugging away at regal Dwarf armour. There were so many suits to be designed, but he steadfastly waded through, securing sign-off after sign-off from Peter and turning amazing design after amazing design over to our Weta Workshop floor staff to prototype and build.

Richard Taylor,
Weta Workshop Design & Special Effects Supervisor

The Dwarves' Erebor armour was one of the first things I started playing with, throwing out a whole bunch of different ideas around the notion of hard-edged, geometric armour. None of it was character-specific when I began. I was just exploring shapes and trying to figure out how far we could push them in various directions.

We started calling the designs I was coming up with regal armour because the armour our characters would wear at this point had to have a very rich, regal quality to it, as if the Dwarves had pulled it out of the Dragon hoard. It would look at home amongst the treasure. These suits were the armour of past kings, princes and lords, with precious metals, beautiful finishes and exquisite decoration. The book refers to the Dwarves as gleaming in the sunlight, wearing shining armour, so that was the image I had in my mind and why the first concepts were all in the range of gold and copper, rich metal colours.

Nick Keller, Weta Workshop Designer

NK
WW

NK
WW

NK
WW

NK
WW

NK/ST
WW

NK/ST
WW

NK/ST
WW

We were a significant portion of the way into building our regal armour when the question about whether the Dwarves would actually wear this armour in battle came up. Peter, Fran and Philippa were re-examining the way the scenes unfolded and had come to the conclusion that there was something thematically engaging about the Dwarves removing their regal trappings and going into battle less armoured and perhaps with a little more humility. It would mean they would look like more of a fast-moving, lightly armoured team rather than gilded tanks. Everyone loved the regal armour we had been developing, and it would still have its place in the story, but now it would be something the Dwarves put on to appear in glory and splendour atop the parapets rather than charge into battle beneath.

Richard Taylor,
Weta Workshop Design & Special Effects Supervisor

JH
AD

JH
AD

NK
WW

THORIN'S REGAL ARMOUR & WEAPONS

One of the concepts in our first round of nonspecific regal Dwarf armour had a ram motif in it. The helmet had stylized curling rams' horns around the face. When we started thinking about assigning armour to certain characters this one ended up going on Thorin.

We took the golden ram armour concept a long way and even created a working prototype suit that Richard Armitage tried on. At some point there was some re-evaluation of the motif and whether the ram was meaningful enough. That led to some experimentation with other motifs that could replace it. It might seem a bit counterintuitive, but Peter, Fran and Philippa asked to see some exploration around a possible Dragon motif in the armour, which I guess was a literal way of showing the Dragon-sickness overtaking Thorin.

NK
WW

Ultimately it was a raven motif that was settled upon. The Dwarves of Erebor had a close relationship with the ravens of the Mountain in the book so it made sense that they might feature in their works. It also became an interesting contrast that we could explore, having shiny black panels alternating with the polished gold.

The perched raven helmet was an 'out there' design, and in the end it was ditched in preference for a crown, which actually made more sense from a story point of view.

Our thinking about Thorin was that by this point in the story his obsession with reclaiming the gold and treasure was becoming a sickness, an infatuation, so I thought it could be interesting to have him literally wear gold. With that in mind the armour was intended to be a gleaming gold from head to foot. I had played it a little safe in the early artwork but the feedback we got was to push it to an extreme, so as we went along the gold got brighter and brighter, becoming a very bold, gleaming yellow-gold by the time we had settled on the raven as the dominant motif in the armour.

Nick Keller, Weta Workshop Designer

The crown Thorin wore was in fact the same design as the one worn by his grandfather, Thror. We designed the armour to be the same for both characters too, the idea being that, upon reclaiming the Mountain from Smaug, Thorin was putting on Thror's armour and taking on the same sickness that affected his grandfather. It couldn't be exactly the same suit or crown because Thror was wearing it when he fought outside Moria, but we rationalized that he had more than one and it was left behind when they fled from Erebor. Now Thorin was reclaiming his legacy and taking on his grandfather's mantle, and his affliction.

The black in the armour could be interpreted as the growing darkness of his character, something Philippa said, but it was also a happy accident, because it looked so cool with the gold.

Nick Keller, Weta Workshop Designer

Like his armour, Thorin's sword was based on the same design as his grandfather's, polished steel with an inlaid gold core to the blade and decorative elements of black stone like obsidian, which we veined with ripples of white. The final prop that our armour and weapons team at Weta Workshop made was a stunning weapon, but so broad that the scabbard would have to be huge. Rather than have a big flat slab of leather we chose to make it more like an open holster. It was something we did with the Elves and a few of the Dwarf weapons as well, having an open side that revealed the blade, even when sheathed. Historically, some of the big two-handed swords that might be slung across someone's back were carried in simple, open scabbards so there was some precedent, and it looked much better than having a huge, wide scabbard.

Nick Keller, Weta Workshop Designer

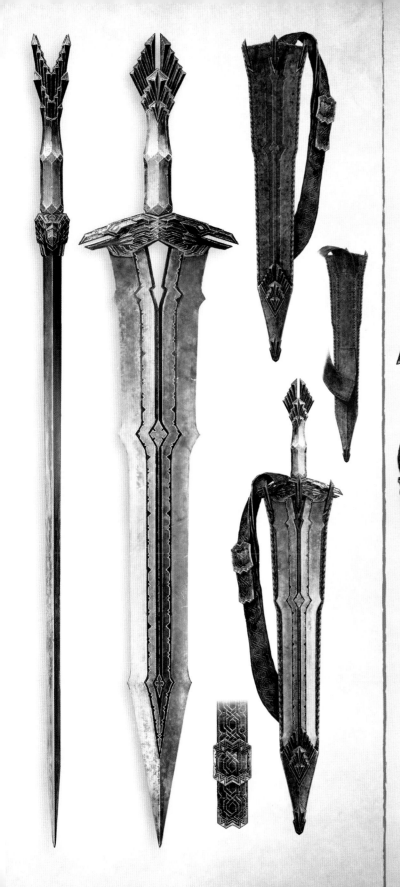

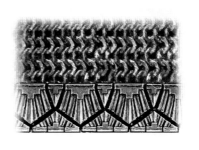

Fili & Kili's Regal Armour & Weapons

We were fortunate enough to get some of our regal armour designs just right with the first pass, but others were harder. Fili's was among the more difficult to achieve. Peter wanted a powerful simplicity that would still feel noble, and that was surprisingly complex to get right. We ultimately made and remade his armour a couple of times before we were satisfied that we had achieved what was called for in the brief. The fittings had to happen while location filming was going on, so our Weta Workshop Costume Supervisor Matt Appleton, Specialty Costume Maker Alistair McDougall and I flew to the South Island and drove out to the often remarkable and remote locations where filming was going on to conduct our fitting tests with the director and actors, taking lots of photographs and notes to bring back with us and make alterations back at the workshop.

Richard Taylor,
Weta Workshop Design & Special Effects Supervisor

I wanted to put helmets on all the Dwarves to begin with, because that would make sense in the kind of battle situation they were going to find themselves in. As tended to happen with most main characters, those helmets came off and we started to strip back how much we dressed them in. Although I designed one for him, in the end Kili didn't end up with a helmet at all. It's understandable because the audience needs to be able to see their faces easily and not have something interfering with how their performances come across.

Nick Keller, Weta Workshop Designer

With Fili I thought it would be interesting to explore a kind of brigandine tunic, something that we hadn't really much seen in Middle-earth up till now. I had done a lot of plate armour on other characters so the chance to try something new seemed like a good opportunity. Being a young, agile character a lighter, more streamlined armour made sense too, as it would permit more movement.

A decorative precedent had been set with Gimli's appearance in *The Lord of the Rings*, which we followed on these films. Dwarves like their elaborate, angular knot-work. I ended up drawing a lot of Celtic-inspired knot-work between the regal Dwarf armour, Iron Hills and Erebor Dwarf armies, going in different directions to create signature patterns for certain characters, particularly on belts and buckles.

Nick Keller, Weta Workshop Designer

As I was drawing armour I was also thinking about accompanying weapons – what kind of fighting styles might the various weapons or configurations suggest? We were throwing ideas at the wall to see what would stick. How about a sword and shield, or twin small axes, or a mace, or a two-handed sword? Unique weapons and fighting styles were ways we could distinguish different Dwarves. Fili's sword was an attempt to create a Dwarven two-handed sword, something big and broad.

Nick Keller, Weta Workshop Designer

NK
WW

At one point Kili's armour ended up with a suggestion of muscle groups in its form. I was asked to explore something with Romanesque references, but with a more abstract, typically Dwarven, angular treatment.

Nick Keller, Weta Workshop Designer

We realized that we were losing Kili's natural power and grace under the heavy plate armour. The more we looked at him in the sculpted chest and belly plates the more we knew we were drifting off from who the character was. Kili just wasn't that complicated or the kind of Dwarf who would think so much of himself as to wear something like that. His simpler sensibility suited a less elaborate armour design, which ultimately resulted in us stripping him back to a long shirt of gold chain and exposing his arms.

Richard Taylor,
Weta Workshop Design & Special Effects Supervisor

The chestplate we had been pursuing for Kili was dropped in favour of chain, which would be less bulky or restrictive, but we retained the pauldrons on his shoulders with a scale-like construction that were similar to Dwalin's and worked very well as a practical build. There is always the risk when building something quite bulky, as Dwarven designs tended to be, that they can be difficult to articulate successfully so it was great to find that these actually worked very well.

Kili's sword was inspired by the thought of making a weapon that looked almost architectural, a single hand grip or possibly a hand-and-a-half sword.

Nick Keller, Weta Workshop Designer

DWALIN'S REGAL ARMOUR & WEAPONS

The final armour Dwalin wore was one of my favourites. I would have loved to have seen him wear it in battle, but it was still just so cool to see the actor wearing it as a full, working suit of armour. It started out as bluish in the first images because the armour had been that colour when drawn first for no specific Dwarf. Once it became Dwalin's armour we shifted the colour to be more in keeping with what was established for him.

With the green theme in his armour Peter looked at Dwalin's battle axe and suggested that we should give it blades that were made out of greenstone, or jade. In New Zealand it is called *pounamu* and it has cultural significance and value. The Maori people, native to New Zealand, carve it into jewellery and also make weapons out of it. It's a beautiful stone, translucent and with flecks and veins of colour through it, so it made for a very eye-catching weapon. People from outside New Zealand probably wouldn't catch the reference, and the films are fantasy after all, but for those of us who know what greenstone is and its specialness here it was cool to see Dwalin wielding an axe made of it.

A dagger for Dwalin came through as a fairly late request, but having just designed his greenstone axe it made sense to have it match.

Over his chestplate I gave Dwalin a set of crisscrossing bandoliers to wear that would hold a pair of axes on his back. It was a conscious choice to recreate that strong silhouette he had in the first film with his paired axes that were harnessed the same way. The bandolier was a new design, but very similar to what he wore at the beginning of the journey, before the Dwarves lost all their stuff. Like his big double-headed axe we imagined the two he wore on his back as being the same kind of stone.

Nick Keller, Weta Workshop Designer

BALIN'S REGAL ARMOUR & WEAPONS

Balin's regal costume was influenced by Roman legionnaires' armour, but reinterpreted with Dwarven shape language, very regimented looking. Red, being Balin's signature colour, came through in the undergarments. Colour was something that came towards the end of the design phase for each suit of armour. Because they each evolved out of concepts that weren't specifically designed with a character in mind and were then allocated to named Dwarves I began by simply superimposing our actors' faces in the generic armour. Some of them changed and were swapped around. Kili's first suit ended up going to Oin, for example. As we then started to develop each suit of armour and tailor it to specific Dwarves we honed in on colours that suited them as well. While I didn't literally lift these colours from their travelling costumes, I did have those costumes in mind, so where colour has crept in it often nods at what was established for that Dwarf in the very first film. Sometimes these were subtle, and sometimes, as with Balin, they were more obvious.

Nick Keller, Weta Workshop Designer

Ori, Dori & Nori's Regal Armour & Weapons

Dori's weapon grew out of an early unassigned regal Dwarf mace, but with lengthened spikes to make it look more dangerous.

We had a grab bag of weapons that I had come up with which Peter liked. I started throwing them at different Dwarves to see which felt appropriate, and Nori ended up with a huge mace. There were some similarities in the sharp angles and shapes of the weapon and his fancy hair-do, so it fit well in that respect. The mace began as a smaller one-handed weapon but grew to something that probably demands two hands. We also had a regal shield for Nori to use in his other hand, but that's a little trickier with such a huge mace.

It was a conscious decision to offer something completely different and much more kick-ass for Ori to use than the little knife and slingshot he had carried thus far. So I gave him a giant axe!

Nick Keller, Weta Workshop Designer

A request came in at one point for us to whip up some concepts for a new slingshot for Ori. The idea was that he would find a brand new, fancy one in the treasure hoard of Erebor. All the Dwarves were getting impressive new weapons to match their regal armour, so my approach was to imagine a slingshot made for a young Dwarven prince. I could imagine how excited Ori would be to come across it.

We were in the midst of designing Dwarven war chariots so the obvious choice for me was to design it with a pair of stylized ram's horns forming the V. I created two versions, the second ditching the horn idea and going with some elegant Dwarven patterning instead, which was ultimately the favourite.

Paul Tobin, Weta Workshop Designer

I wanted Dori and Nori's helmets to have a similar design aesthetic, with radial blade-like projections. Dori's armour had a lot of similarities to Balin's and in fact shared some common parts, but a different colour did a lot to make them seem more different than they were. The purple in his garments linked with the colours he wore in his travelling costume, and this became stronger as we went along. The first concepts were quite muted with just hints of colour for each character, but it was a good way of distinguishing them so we became bolder with its use in the regal armour later in the design and manufacturing phase.

Nick Keller, Weta Workshop Designer

Adding scalemaille was another way of making Dori's armour unique, so he has a skirt of pointed scales as well as sleeves and panels that hang from his helmet on either side of his face. The spiky shapes in Ori's mace were echoed in his helmet, preserving the continuity of that silhouette.

Nori had a wide belt of interlocking metal pieces. It was something I was exploring for the cool visual it gave us and ended up on a few of the other Dwarves as well, including Dain. Nori's armour proved to be quite tricky to build and have move correctly. While some of the other Dwarves' suits of armour were similar to each other in construction, or aesthetically linked by common elements, Nori's was unique so needed its own problem solving. It had lots of little plain geometric facets, overlaid to articulate over one another, pointing up to create a jagged silhouette. It took some doing but the team building it got it to work and it looked amazing.

Nick Keller, Weta Workshop Designer

Ori's armour was an interesting one because it was a combination of chain and little plates, quite different from most of the other Dwarves' suits. Even the helmet wasn't a solid unit, but something that was essentially pieces held together by chain. The overriding goal with Ori's armour was to have him look overwhelmed and lost in it, so the helmet was a bit too large and hung low over his eyes and the rest of it all hung on him, a bit baggy and loose. Comparing the earlier and later concept art, that choice to make everything bigger and less fitted should be clear. The colour also changed from a coppery-orange to something more reddish with hints of other colours in there.

Nick Keller, Weta Workshop Designer

BIFUR & BOFUR'S REGAL ARMOUR & WEAPONS

By the time I got to Bifur's weapon I must have drawn hundreds of Dwarf axes, so I was hungry for anything I could do to make it look different. The point of difference in this case became the bent, kicked-back neck of the axe, which was a shape that carried over into the regal hammer I was designing simultaneously for Bofur. The characters were cousins so I guess it was nice to get some continuity in there with their weapons.

Nick Keller, Weta Workshop Designer

Bifur and Bofur's helmets share a common design ancestry. Balin's regal helmet was designed first and it established the basis for this particular armour family's aesthetic. Bifur and Bofur's helmets were essentially variations on that design, but Bifur's helmet required a little bit of additional modification in order for it to fit. The idea was that he had found a helmet in the Erebor armoury that he liked and had hacked a hole in it to accommodate the axe-head that was still stuck in his skull.

Nick Keller, Weta Workshop Designer

Bofur's helmet concepts were conceived over the same base as Bifur's and included one crazy idea I threw in for consideration which had these wings that were meant to evoke the same sort of silhouette as the iconic furry hat he had worn throughout the movies. If you saw him on the battlefield, this distinctive shape, hearkening back to the silly hat, would have helped you pick him out of the crowd. Of course, in the end, it was a bit far-fetched. I guess it was a simpler concept for him to still just be wearing his hat instead of having dug out a helmet that looked like it.

Nick Keller, Weta Workshop Designer

Unlike their helmets or weapons, Bifur and Bofur's suits of regal armour were completely different. There were certain elements and motifs that popped up here and there within the families of design in all of the regal armour, but mostly each suit was unique across all thirteen Dwarves. There was a lot of armour to design, but fortunately it was all very enjoyable.

Nick Keller, Weta Workshop Designer

Bombur's Regal Armour & Weapons

Bombur's regal armour and weaponry were great fun to design. I can't recall who first raised it, but it was suggested that he should be in some kind of giant belly plate, essentially turning him into a big ball with arms and legs. I thought it was appropriate to how Bombur's character had been developed that he would reel around the battlefield in this big round steel ball. It was an odd one, conceptually, because it would have to be a custom-built and fitted piece of armour, so we had to assume there was another Dwarf of similar proportions living in Erebor back in the days before Smaug came and Bombur found this suit to be a good fit. Because it was such a large, unarticulated piece of armour I thought it would be better to keep the rest of him relatively unencumbered, so no leg armour that might slow him down. Before the belly plate idea had come up we looked at some other solutions, like the notion that he actually wore two Dwarves' worth of armour, jury-rigging two chainmaille vests together with some belts to cover his tummy. The single belly plate was cooler.

While the initial concept art was brown we ended up changing it to a green and Sourisak Chanpaseuth did an amazing job of painting it, working all these beautifully subtle hints of corrosion and variation into the surface.

Designing the helmets, I kept the faces as open as possible so that the actor's face wasn't obscured and we could read their expressions and features clearly. Carrying on the shapes in his armour, Bombur's helmet was rounded and ended up with a little sculptural wild boar on it as a crest in an effort to give him a distinct silhouette.

Nick Keller, Weta Workshop Designer

I explored a few ideas around the giant horn Bombur was to blow. Might it be metal, intricately fashioned and detailed, or was it the hollowed horn of some kind of giant animal? That idea seemed to work best, so we adopted the notion of it being an animal horn in the main body but with some worked metal elements attached as ornamentation with a Dwarven aesthetic in the design.

Nick Keller, Weta Workshop Designer

NK
WW

One of the last props we built for the movies was the huge horn that Bombur would blow to announce the Dwarves' arrival in the battle. We had only a few days in which to design and construct this piece so where ordinarily we would create a prototype and then mould and cast it out in a lightweight, hollow material in this instance we model-made the actual prop as a one-off piece and carried it to set to be used. It was carved out of blocks of high density foam with urethane, fibreglass and polyester resin and there was some weight to it. We don't like to burden our actors with heavy props but Stephen Hunter was a trooper and looked amazing in his costume with the great spiralling horn mounted off his body, striding to the parapet to blast it.

Richard Taylor,
Weta Workshop Design & Special Effects Supervisor

I liked the idea that Bombur had this giant wrecking ball of a weapon, a big round instrument of destruction that he would be swinging around. As with most of our weapons we presented cardboard mock-ups to Peter at various sizes so he could pick what he felt looked appropriate, ranging from the conservative through significantly larger to the ridiculously big. Peter tended to always favour the bigger ones. We were a bit hesitant in the beginning because they seemed so oversized, but that was also because we were used to thinking in human scale. The Dwarves would be wearing so much make-up, hair and clothing that their shapes were significantly different once fully dressed for the camera, much bigger than a person generally is, so they needed chunky weapons in their hands just to feel balanced.

We also had to think about the fact that they would be shot to be smaller than they really were, so unless their weapons had a significant mass they would just look puny and ineffectual on screen. Hammers in particular were susceptible to looking too small. Ideally you would want a hammer to have a small end so that all the force of the blow was concentrated at the point for maximum impact, but even a good-sized hammer in our hands could look like a toothpick in the hands of a Dwarf on screen, which is why the heads of our hammers tended to be huge. The same was true of the head on Bombur's flail, which crept up in size before we were done.

Nick Keller, Weta Workshop Designer

OIN & GLOIN'S REGAL ARMOUR & WEAPONS

As with all of the Dwarves' regal armour designs, for Oin and Gloin I began with a bunch of concepts that had been developed without specific characters in mind. Once we had a cast confirmed and were getting a sense of who these characters were I started matching existing design concepts with names and adding their faces to my artwork to see how they looked.

There was a particular armour concept that I always really liked and initially I suggested it for Kili. It wasn't quite right for him but it seemed to work on Oin very well. It was interesting to transition from the drawing to a practical, working costume. This one had a very precise arrangement of interlocking plates rigged together with chain, but it worked well in the final suit. The style had historical precedents, but they tended to be quite simple with horizontal or vertical plates. We were trying something a bit more unusual with our hexagons and triangles and other shapes, in order to show off the technical prowess of Dwarven armour-makers, so it was quite complex, but the guys on the Weta Workshop floor did a great job and it looked fantastic.

Nick Keller, Weta Workshop Designer

NK
WW

There were a few of those great full-circle moments on this trilogy that I revelled in, fondly recalling the early days back on *The Lord of the Rings* when we still had no idea what we were getting ourselves into, or what this was all going to become. More than a decade on, revisiting Gimli's original helmet and weapons to extrapolate the look of Gloin's regal armour was one of those times.

Richard Taylor,
Weta Workshop Design & Special Effects Supervisor

I had designed a shield to go with the armour Oin was allocated and by happy accident, when it ended up being assigned to him, the shapes seemed to mirror the forms of his distinctive beard. I also did a little bit of reverse engineering on it to make the look work, but it was a case of a character and armour dovetailing together nicely. The padded, studded suede elements complemented the quilted tunic from his travelling costume. I thought that, in his full armour with sword and shield, Oin had a stately quality.

Gloin began with an armour concept that had been pitched for the Iron Hill Dwarves, and then ended up being adapted and pitched for Thror's armour before ultimately being abandoned completely. The boar motif was very strong in that particular concept, and there was a helmet with feathered crest elements.

Somewhere along the way someone suggested that we should give Gloin the same helmet Gimli wore in *The Lord of the Rings*, suggesting that when Gimli went to Rivendell and ended up joining the Fellowship he had taken his father's old regal helmet. It was such a cool idea and a great way to establish another link between the trilogies, so then we decided to design a whole suit of armour based on the helmet.

That was a fun design task, creating a new suit of armour but harmonizing it with the iconography and shapes of a helmet devised more than a decade ago. We pushed the colours a little brighter and stronger, rationalizing that by the time Gimli wore the helmet years later it had dulled and the leather had desaturated, but essentially all the shape-language, decorative details and colours in the armour came from either the helmet or the axes that Gimli and Gloin both carried. We beefed up the reddish-brown and gold a bit so that it had the colouring that we had already associated with Gloin and to keep it as bright and colourful as the other regal armour. Again, the suit worked very well as a practical costume too. I think Gloin must have had a spare axe stashed somewhere in the Mountain, or maybe that style wasn't unique to the ones he carried and lost in the journey to get there.

Nick Keller, Weta Workshop Designer

COMPANY OF THORIN
BATTLE ARMOUR & COSTUMES

NK
WW

NK
WW

NK
WW

BB
CD

NK
WW

For a long time it looked like the Dwarves of Thorin's Company would be fighting in their full regal armour. When the choice was made by the filmmakers to strip them out of this and garb them in lighter, less military costumes it gave us the opportunity to combine elements from what we called Stage 1 Erebor, their reclaimed Erebor costumes, and the regal armour designed and built at Weta Workshop, mixing them to create something new. The battle costumes were more than simple combinations, however. We designed them as whole costumes, in some cases almost entirely new, others incorporating the majority of their elements from the earlier designs.

Bob Buck, Costume Designer

Gloin returned to his design roots with colours and shapes in his battle costume very reminiscent of his clothing from *An Unexpected Journey*. We slipped some more burgundy into the palette and used velvet to suggest a richer garment with lots of three-dimensional detail over suede and leather. His costume was fitted, with some simple, elegant fittings down the front and a belt that recycled motifs from Gimli's costume in metal panels.

Bob Buck, Costume Designer

The idea with most of the battle costumes was that they were what the Dwarves were wearing underneath their regal armour, so once they had shucked off their major hard armour components, this would be what they looked like. There were still elements of chain and some hard armour pieces, gloves and greaves, but for the most part they were less heavily armoured and weighted down. We worked very closely with Bob Buck, the Costume Designer at 3Foot7's Costume Department. In some cases the leads were taken from Bob's designs for the Dwarves' Erebor reclaimed outfits, the Stage 1 Erebor costumes. The regal armour was Stage 2 and these battle costumes were Stage 3. Bob took cues off some of the regal armour and I cued off some of his concepts, and we worked back and forth, divvying up Dwarves between

us to have a go at and sometimes working over the top of each other's concepts as well. It was very collaborative. It was an exercise in working backwards from the regal designs while still creating what looked like full costumes. It was a bit tricky, to be honest, working backwards that way, stripping away elements without losing what was working.

Nick Keller, Weta Workshop Designer

There was the notion that essentially these battle costumes should appear to be what they were wearing under their regal armour, even if in truth that was not the case, but they represented an extrapolation of the same train of thought that began with the reclaimed Erebor and regal armour costumes.

One benefit of removing the heavy armour was that the thirteen Dwarves now looked very different from the ranks of Iron Hill soldiers and Dain. They became more of a militia, a fast-moving, non-regimental force of agile warriors rather than armoured troops.

Bob Buck, Costume Designer

The golden boy of our merry band, Kili was dressed in a hauberk of golden chain, a rich and princely garment that was both tough and regal at the same time. Underneath this he would wear a beautiful rich turquoise-blue garment with quilted sleeves. Rather than button him up tight we left Kili's vest open, as if it was put on without much effort. He might wear fine clothing, but Kili wasn't a fussy character.

In battle Bifur wore a variant on his reclaimed Erebor costume with armour elements introduced, including chain sleeves, an interesting and textured mix of military and civilian working-man wear.

Bob Buck, Costume Designer

I envisioned Bombur's battle costume as a combination of heavy leathers and suede, studded with ornamental bits and pieces, and with an interlocking chain belt around the whole thing.

Nick Keller, Weta Workshop Designer

Weta Workshop has enjoyed a long working relationship with Bob Buck, who by the third film of *The Hobbit* was the Costume Designer at 3Foot7. I first worked with Bob way back in the days of *Hercules: The Legendary Journeys*. During *The Lord of the Rings* Bob was a member of our leather- and armour-making team for a while, so it was great to see him taking on costume design responsibilities at this most challenging time on *The Hobbit*. It was a time of great pressure, but going down to 3Foot7 for meetings with the filmmakers and Bob was always a pleasure thanks to Bob's high-spirited approach and great sense of humour. We worked very closely together on the Dwarves' daunting Erebor and battle costumes and armour. There's nothing like a good laugh with colleagues at the seemingly insurmountable workload ahead to make taking those first steps easier.

Richard Taylor,
Weta Workshop Design & Special Effects Supervisor

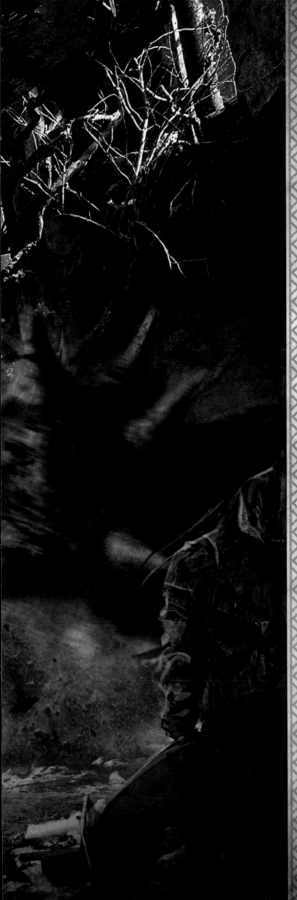

FOUL THINGS

THE ORC HOST

Leading an army of Orcs out of Dol Guldur, Azog the Defiler lays siege to Erebor and the refugees taking shelter in Dale. In his host of foul creatures are Orcs, Trolls of diverse kinds, Wargs armoured for battle, and worse things still. Azog's son Bolg arrives late to the melee with an army of his own from the Orc fortress of Gundabad, accompanied by a swarm of killer bats.

In the earliest days the dark forces were to be Goblins and Wargs. In Tolkien's books Goblins are synonymous with Orcs, but as the scripts evolved and the Goblins came to be characterized as a smaller, in-bred rabble rather than regimented military and but one of several races of Orcs, the need for Azog's warriors to be of a larger, more intimidating variety became apparent. Azog had been established as a giant Gundabad Orc, so it made sense to distinguish this new breed of powerfully built Orcs as being of his kind.

The perennial question of whether the Orc army would be achieved entirely or in part with digital technology, or be physically costumed and masked actors, was an open one with an answer that changed more than once during the long design and manufacture phases, affecting the direction and constraints of the designs undertaken. What was never in question was whether the many horrific war beasts that would accompany Azog's hordes would be anything but computer generated. Yet exactly what the make-up of this nightmarish menagerie would be took some time to nail down, resulting in several rounds of enjoyable monster design for the creature team.

AZOG'S ORC SOLDIERS

CREATURE DESIGNS

JB
WW

JB
WW

JB
WW

GJH
WW

JB
WW

JB/GT
WW

DM
WW

JB
WW

Whether sculpting with Plasticine, ZBrush modelling or painting in Photoshop, I think everyone within our design studio had a go at the big new Orcs of Azog's army. At one time we were briefed with the requirement that this breed of Orc warriors would be realized with traditional prosthetics worn by costumed human performers, but as the film progressed it became apparent that a mixture of both physical and digital solutions would be used, which freed us to push our designs further into extremes because we were no longer beholden to accommodating the locked features of the human face. Unless we were to embrace animatronics (which we did look into), a prosthetic make-up is limited in how far it can stray from human proportions by the triangle of the two eyes and mouth. Those distances can't change, so the creature will always have them in common with a human, and being an additive process, a prosthetic creature's forehead can never be smaller than the performer's, its nose never flatter than the person's.

A completely digital creature faces no such restrictions so we could slope the forehead, widen eyes, enlarge mouths and push the proportions of our new Orcs to inhuman extremes. A broad range of conceptual ideas were explored and these were carefully viewed and selected by Peter, with his favourites being sent through to Weta Digital for them to begin the modelling of these characters.

Richard Taylor,
Weta Workshop Design & Special Effects Supervisor

I had the bodyguard of Bolg in mind when I started sculpting maquettes for the Orcs, big, burly characters that were much bigger than most of the Orcs we'd seen till this point. Tolkien mentioned these big Goblin-men amongst the rest of the horde, so that was what I had in mind. One of them I gave six fingers, another one an extra nipple, just trying to work in little ideas like perhaps they were inbred.

The way a lot of Tolkien's characterizations of Orcs read, there's a certain East-End London thug-thing going on, so I couldn't help but think of some of the characters like Lenny McLean's Barry the Baptist from *Lock, Stock and Two Smoking Barrels*, and channel a little of that into my sculpts – great faces.

I had a Beorn concept that Peter liked, but not so much for Beorn as for an Orc, some kind of giant Gundabad Orc. Peter was keen on the idea of there being a few very, very big Orcs, so we took the beard and hair off and I worked back into it to turn it into an Orc concept (*overleaf, bottom left*).

Jamie Beswarick, Weta Workshop Designer & Sculptor

While we had started out thinking of the different breeds of Orcs as having distinct builds and features, the Gundabad or soldier Orcs being big, hulking characters and the hunters being a smaller, more weasely-featured gang, in the end things became more blended together.

Greg Tozer, Weta Workshop Designer

AJB
WW

AJB
WW

AJB
WW

AJB
WW

GT
WW

GT
WW

GT
WW

GT
WW

GT
WW

GT
WW

GT
WW

JB
WW

GT
WW

GT
WW

GT
WW

GT
WW

GT
WW

PT
WW

PT
WW

PT
WW

DF
WW

GT
WW

GT
WW

GT
WW

SS
WW

GT
WW

GT
WW

JB/GT
WW

GT
WW

GT
WW

Azog's Orc Soldiers

ARMOUR & WEAPONS

One of the main thrusts for us in the beginning of the development of the Orc army was to find a strong helmet shape or shapes, because that tends to be one of the most defining elements in any suit of armour. Their weapons would ideally echo that same shape as well. Fortunately the broad, flat axe-head shape, championed by John Howe, established itself as a signature for these guys. It was present in some of the earliest explorations we made and the motif carried right through. Repeating it helped establish a sense of uniformity, so we reused it again and again, in helmet crests, cheek guards, weapons, shoulder plates, greaves, chest plates or shields.

Paul Tobin, Weta Workshop Designer

NK
WW

NK
WW

PT
WW

PT
WW

PT
WW

PT
WW

GJH
WW

JH
WD

GH
WW

GH
WW

NK
WW

The Orc soldiers' armour was being designed for a long time. We kept coming back to it, but I was pleased that a lot of the iconic shapes that appeared very early on stuck and came all the way through to the final selection. In the end we had a selection of around half a dozen strong helmet shapes that we created variations on. The directive was to generate an assortment of different looks that all felt like they came from the same design family. The brief was to find a combination of militaristic uniformity, like the Uruk-hai had in *The Lord of the Rings*, and more of a wild and barbarian rabble like the Mordor Orcs. I got the impression the Orc soldiers of *The Hobbit* would sit somewhere in the middle, between these extremes, but they needed to have the feel of a serious army, a force to be reckoned with. We had repetitive armour components that all the soldiers would have in common, but then mixed in some variation, mostly in the helmets.

Nick Keller, Weta Workshop Designer

NK
WW

The Dwarf heads on spikes (*overleaf*) was one of Peter's ideas that came up early on. We were happy to run with it because it was a cool look – very dramatic. Amongst the design team at Weta Workshop we thought maybe the number of heads each soldier carried on his back denoted how accomplished a warrior he was. The more senior an Orc was, the more trophies he had on his rig.

Nick Keller, Weta Workshop Designer

We went all over the place as we tried to figure out what colours could represent the signature palette for Azog's soldiers, who, at the time, we were calling the Gundabad Orcs. Peter wanted them to have a distinct colour identity. We had seen so many other Orc breeds by this point that it was important to understand that these guys were something new. We explored a matte blackened, almost burnt finish as well as some that pushed into iridescent colours. There was the plain Uruk-hai gun-metal grey look, but then we also tried some really far-out colour schemes, like copper patinas that pushed into turquoise and acid-green, corroded metal colours.

The red look was something we were playing with for Azog or Bolg at the time, which was very strong. The blood-red contrasted with a different kind of copper patina base colour on the armour plate underneath. Copper patinas can run the gamut from yellowy-green right through to a blue. These concepts were at the cyan-blue end of the spectrum. I think that might have been my favourite of the schemes that we explored. I would have loved to have seen the entire army looking like they had buckets of scarlet blood dumped over them before going into battle.

Nick Keller, Weta Workshop Designer

NK
WW

JH
WD

AZOG

Peter talked to us about giving Azog some armour when he turned up at the Battle of the Five Armies. I put him in a suit of full plate armour in my first piece of artwork (*left*) because I thought it would be cool to create a strong contrast against his stripped-back appearance in the first two films. Peter didn't feel him being so armoured fit with Azog's persona. All the scarification on his skin was something Azog showed off. He didn't wear any protection because he was so supremely confident in his superiority, so covering him in plate from head to toe didn't ring true for who he was.

Instead we moved forward by putting just a few minimal components on him. It represented a difference to his bare-chested look but he was still recognizable in an instant. That was also why we looked at white armour, carrying through the colour of his skin to keep him distinct from everyone else.

The helmets I came up with for Azog had a skull-like thing going on. I wanted to keep it fairly simple and skull references are an easy way to introduce a bit of bad-assness.

I looked at what Azog might do with his severed arm, too. At first I was thinking he might have some kind of socket that he would slot his skewer-arm into, but Peter liked the idea of something much more visceral. Wearing something on top, Azog would instead actually tear his old hook out of his arm and replace it with a new appendage more suited for war.

Nick Keller, Weta Workshop Designer

Azog controls the battle from his vantage point atop the ruined fortress of Ravenhill. Peter wanted a signal system for Azog to use to direct the movements of his troops, so we could identify the flow of his forces down below with the directions he was giving from on high. I came up with these big burning totems that would glow through the low cloud shrouding the tower, because Ravenhill is in mist.

Alan Lee, Concept Art Director

AL
WD

NK
WW

NK
WW

BOLG

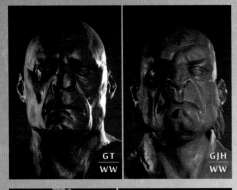

It is always Peter's desire that we find memorable and unique characters through our design work. Because the Orcs were a rabble – muddy, bloody and dressed in scraps and ragged armour – they ran the risk of all blending into one and being indistinguishable to audiences. The filmmakers felt very strongly that featured Orcs like Bolg and Azog needed very strong design icons to define them against the backdrop of their minions.

Bolg's final look actually came out of earlier concepts for Azog that became available when Azog's character was redefined in the scripts. That is why he ended up with the metal cage on his head, an idea that came out of the reference in the books to Azog having a huge, iron-clad head. Peter didn't want just another helmet design, so that became a directive to do something new. Bolg was to be Azog's son and, at the time, the keeper of the dungeons in the Necromancer's fortress of Dol Guldur, a gloomy, forbidding place, so we imagined that the aggressive and unique look of the character with his bold splashes of red would help him pop against dark backgrounds.

Richard Taylor,
Weta Workshop Design & Special Effects Supervisor

With Bolg, the challenge for me as a recent addition to the sculpting and design team was to come up with something new. Considering how many Orcs Weta had created for *The Lord of the Rings* it was daunting to try to come up with something completely original, and yet which was still an Orc. My background includes a lot of paleontological reconstruction work for museums, so I think of myself more as a creature sculptor than a monster-maker. Probably for that reason, when approaching Bolg I gave my conceptual sculpts for his physical make-up a feline, almost leonine, quality, but buried it beneath a layer of scarring and malice. His bone structure was almost noble, but the surface – the muscles, expression and skin – were all grotesque.

Actor Conan Stevens, who at the time would be wearing the prosthetics we were designing, also influenced the sculpture. Thinking about how he would drive the character's expressions through the prosthetic, I used his own facial geometry as a guide, building Bolg's muscles, lines and bone structure off Conan's (*left, middle*).

Peter liked what we had and had the idea of adding an extra layer of horror by encasing Bolg's head in a metal cage, a hideous contraption that was holding his skull together in the wake of some severe trauma, an injury I presumed he might have sustained fighting at the Gates of Moria.

Steven Saunders, Weta Workshop Sculptor

Bolg's costume evolved during fittings, changing direction a few times. Something that I was pleased to see come back in the costume towards the end of the process were the bear claws on his shoulders. They were in our earliest Azog concepts and gave him both a distinctive silhouette and a thematic link to Beorn. We got the impression the two had a history that wasn't too pleasant.

We had been playing with strong colour statements on our new Orc Warg-riders (*above*), trying to find a way to make them different to the predominantly brown and grey Orcs we had seen before. The red pigment made a particularly bold statement so for a time it became our signature colour for Bolg, matting his hair together into blood-red dreadlocks. We also experimented with giving him a beard, something that would have been fairly unique among Orcs.

Though it would change before the final movie, for much of the design phase Bolg had inherited Azog's weapon concepts, including large scimitars and swords, as well as a huge mace that everyone loved. We used a lot of bone in his armour, carrying it through into his weapons. Bone was something we hadn't much seen when Bolg was first being designed, though it has since ended up being a feature of the Orcs in *The Hobbit*.

Nick Keller, Weta Workshop Designer

NK
WW

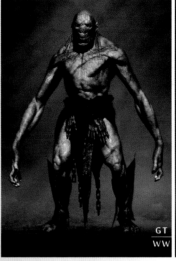

Peter's thinking on Bolg continued to evolve and by the time we got close to him appearing in the second film he had decided that he wanted the character to be entirely digital. It freed his proportions from having to conform to a human shape, so we could go a lot more extreme with our designs, and come up with something fresh whilst maintaining some of the icons that had been already established for the character through the design process up to this stage. One of those was the metal-caged face, and also the idea of some form of extreme disfigurement. Peter wanted to take those characteristics and push them toward something more drastic that affected the entire silhouette of the character.

Andrew Baker, Weta Workshop Designer

AJB
WW

PT
WW

PT
WW

PT
WW

AJB
WW

GT
WW

PT
WW

GT/PT
WW

There were aspects of Bolg's look that we explored which referenced his relationship to Azog, his father. Some of our concepts looked a lot more like Azog than the final design did, but in general the notion was that he was a bit more tormented. We played around with lots of deformities and very nasty looking scars that would establish the character immediately on screen and make him stand out from the rest. It was about making a drastic statement, something quite repulsive that audiences would remember – poor old Bolg.

Andrew Baker, Weta Workshop Designer

Some of the concepts we offered up for Bolg at this time ended up getting recycled back into the pool to be considered for other Orcs. Peter liked them, suggesting they could be an elite guard of some kind, but didn't feel they were exactly what he was looking for in Bolg (*NK images, facing page*).

Nick Keller, Weta Workshop Designer

Making Bolg digital meant we could push his physique in new directions. We lengthened his arms, shortened his legs and made him quite bulky. We also tried some concepts in which he was quite lean and stripped back. The main point of consideration for us was how he compared to Azog. They had to be distinct. Azog was so pristine, symmetrical and healthy-looking, so the natural thing to try was the opposite of that, but rather than sickly we made Bolg corrupt-looking. We discussed the idea that perhaps his proximity to the Necromancer was having an effect on him, so even though he was alive Bolg was decaying.

Greg Tozer, Weta Workshop Designer

Peter liked the rotting nose, dead eye and shredded lips of one of my Bolg Photoshop portraits and this became our lead. Greg Tozer worked up an excellent version of it in ZBrush, a digital sculpting program we use a lot at Weta Workshop, while the cast-off concepts were recycled back into the generic Orc pool. Together with the metal-encased skull that was biting deep into the outline of his head, his ruined features served to make Bolg look appropriately hideous, but at the same time we were careful not to make him seem decrepit or weak with them. He had to be powerful.

Paul Tobin, Weta Workshop Designer

The trick with Bolg was preserving some sense of a relationship to Azog, because the characters are supposed to be father and son, but not making Bolg just a repeat of his dad. Carrying the pale skin through was one way of doing it. As a point of difference we played around for a little while with the concept of tattoos on Bolg. The bone motif kept coming back in his armour and weapons, whether literally bones incorporated into his armour somehow or metal shapes that recalled ribs and vertebrae. It was an association that was reinforced by Bolg being from Dol Guldur, an undead place littered with bones and death.

Paul Tobin, Weta Workshop Designer

Peter asked us to think about Bolg being stripped down in terms of how much he would wear during the second film, but then perhaps put on a few more armour components when we would see him in battle in the third, without completely changing his costume. The thought of something that looked like a ribcage wrapping around his chest was an idea that had stayed with us since some of the earliest drawings in which he literally wore someone else's bones, but it evolved into him having metal armour that looked like ribs, and having them actually embedded in his flesh.

We were all a bit tentative about that directive from Peter at first because we couldn't quite figure out how that would

practically work. We tried doing things like pinning it to his sternum as an anchor point at the front, but keeping the sides free of his skin so his muscles could work underneath, but Peter was adamant he wanted it embedded all the way round, running right under Bolg's arms. It was one of those times you remind yourself you're working on a fantasy film and you can afford to depart from reality for the sake of a strong visual statement. He was a digital character so we could push it further than we would have been able to if he was a guy in prosthetics and physical armour.

Nick Keller, Weta Workshop Designer

Even as a digital character, I still tried to imbue some reality in there by suggesting that the insides of Bolg's arms were lacerated, infected and diseased from continually cutting himself on his own armour.

Nick Keller, Weta Workshop Designer

PT
WW

PT
WW

NK
WW

JH
WD

PT | NK
WW | WW

NK
WW

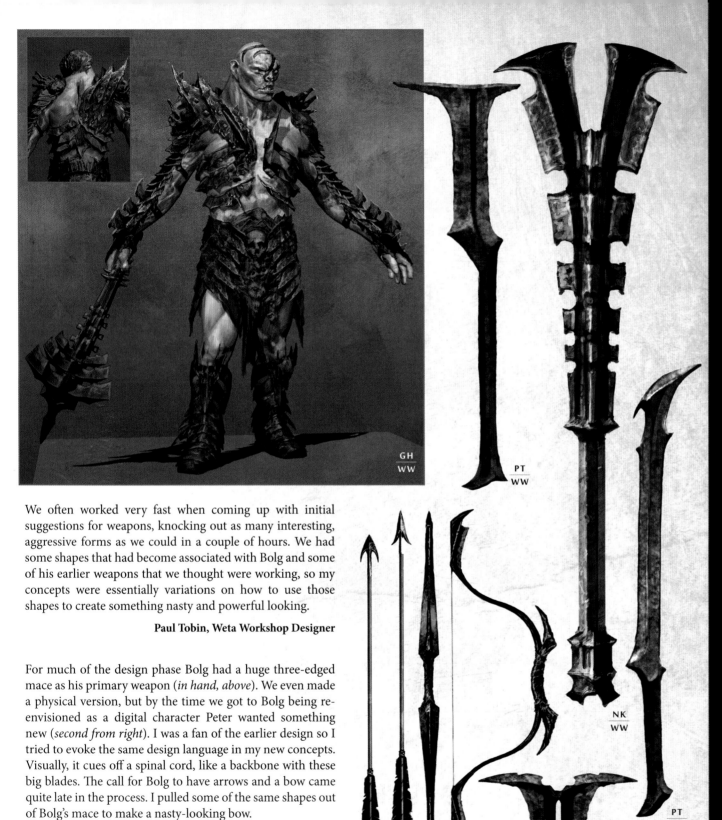

We often worked very fast when coming up with initial suggestions for weapons, knocking out as many interesting, aggressive forms as we could in a couple of hours. We had some shapes that had become associated with Bolg and some of his earlier weapons that we thought were working, so my concepts were essentially variations on how to use those shapes to create something nasty and powerful looking.

Paul Tobin, Weta Workshop Designer

For much of the design phase Bolg had a huge three-edged mace as his primary weapon (*in hand, above*). We even made a physical version, but by the time we got to Bolg being re-envisioned as a digital character Peter wanted something new (*second from right*). I was a fan of the earlier design so I tried to evoke the same design language in my new concepts. Visually, it cues off a spinal cord, like a backbone with these big blades. The call for Bolg to have arrows and a bow came quite late in the process. I pulled some of the same shapes out of Bolg's mace to make a nasty-looking bow.

Nick Keller, Weta Workshop Designer

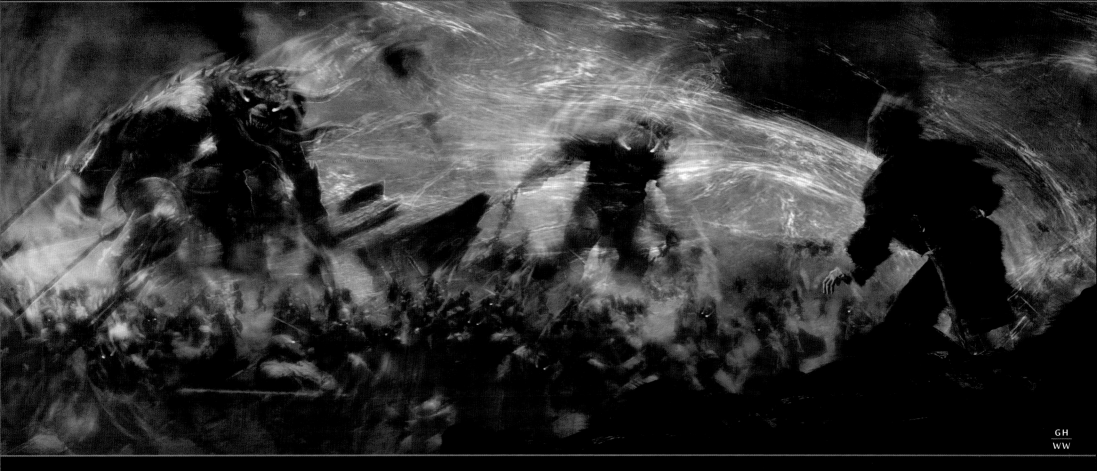

Ring-world Battle

Peter asked to see some ideas for how the battle might appear from the perspective of Bilbo wearing the One Ring. We had seen Ringwraiths and Elves in Ring-world in *The Lord of the Rings*, but we had never seen a massive battle. I was interested to explore what the bad guys might look like. Maybe the Orcs and Trolls' eyes would glow, or perhaps they were fighting but somehow the spiritual outlines of their bodies or faces might turn and respond as the Ring went past them, sensing Bilbo in some way, but not seeing anything. A Warg might be facing away, eating his victim, but then his spirit face would turn and glare in Bilbo's direction, sensing something subconsciously.

Gus Hunter, Weta Workshop Designer

What would a battle look like to Bilbo when he was in Ring-world? He was wearing the Ring so he could move through the battle without detection, but we were thinking that perhaps on some non-physical level the evil spirits within the creatures might be aware of him and react as he went past. The Orcs themselves wouldn't be consciously aware, but the evil that was driving them, that part of Sauron or Morgoth or whatever Dark Power was motivating them, might be subconsciously affected by the Ring's proximity.

Andrew Baker, Weta Workshop Designer

How tragic would it be for Bilbo to witness death in battle while in the Ring-world environment? I thought it might be interesting to see what happens when an Elf is killed, to see the glow fade from them and then witness the spirit departing from its body. In contrast with the light of the Elves, I really liked the idea of being able to see the dark demon forms inside the Wargs and the Orcs.

Greg Tozer, Weta Workshop Designer

NK
WW

We needed some really big, nasty Orcs that were a tangential breed, different from the rest of the soldier Orcs. The brief was that they would be a kind of elite unit that we would see in action at Ravenhill where the final confrontation between Azog and Thorin would take place. I pushed their faces around to try and find a signature look that would help the audience distinguish them from the regular Orc soldiers, flattening their skulls and positioning the eyes higher in the head, which looks more animalistic.

Their armour would have to be distinct from the rank and file troops too, so I tried to find some new shapes. Some of the discarded Bolg designs (*page 200*), that were considered for what we started calling the Berserker Orcs, had armoured chest plates. I thought it could be cool and interesting if they looked like hideous faces with articulated middles that would be like mouths opening and closing.

Nick Keller, Weta Workshop Designer

Orc
Berserkers

The Berserker Orcs, which we liked to think of as the Bodyguard of Bolg, grew out of a need for some kind of creature in the Battle of the Five Armies that was bigger than a regular Orc warrior but not as big as a Troll, something in the eight-foot tall range. Peter wanted there to be a real point of difference between them and the rank and file soldiers. For me it was an opportunity to offer up some incarnations of Sauron or Morgoth's dabblings – things like huge Orcs or Half-Trolls, cunning and cruel beings, intelligent and psychotic killing machines that would be truly frightening.

Greg Tozer, Weta Workshop Designer

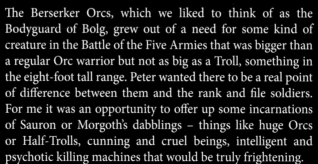

MOUNT GUNDABAD

Mount Gundabad… it is barely mentioned in *The Hobbit*, but when it appeared in the script it was the most exciting of opportunities – to leave Wilderland and go wandering in even more savage climes, far to the north, to the fortress of Gundabad. Where the Grey Mountains dwindle to touch the feet of the Misty Mountains, that is where Mount Gundabad lies, sealing the pass to the Northern Wastes and to Angmar in the north-west. It is from the iron walls of Gundabad that the Orc army marches on the Lonely Mountain.

John Howe, Concept Art Director

I imagined Gundabad to be the shape of a blade, riveted sheets of rusted iron over a skeleton of stone from some elder time, then reaching skyward until it dominated the pass to the North. A defensive structure with the silhouette of a weapon, different from anything else in Middle-earth, backed by vast forges and mines that produce the ore for the Gundabad war machine. Once a Dwarven stronghold, several times lost and retaken during the Second Age, sacred to the Dwarves as the place of awakening of Durin the Deathless, it is now the stronghold of Bolg, son of Azog.

John Howe, Concept Art Director

PT
WW

NK
WW

PT
WW

NK
WW

GT/JH
WW/WD

ORC WAR BEASTS

AL
AD

NK
WW

There had been a precedent set in *The Lord of the Rings* with the beasts that Alan Lee designed to pull the battering ram onto the battlefield (*above, inset*). They had a prehistoric feel to them, as if they were something left over from millennia ago in our own world, but which had survived in Middle-earth. The sabretooth concept (*facing page*) came out of that round of ideas as well, but in the end it didn't go anywhere.

Another cool but dead-end idea was the giant flightless bird (*right, top*), inspired by some of the prehistoric birds from the fossil record. It was partly also a product of desperation! 'What haven't we done yet?'

We yo-yoed back and forth, trying to find something that didn't feel too alien to Middle-earth but was also new. Peter was a bit averse to the prehistoric angle so we abandoned that approach and pursued more fantastical creatures.

Nick Keller, Weta Workshop Designer

I loved the kind of matted fur and wool that bison or musk oxen have when they are moulting, long in some areas and shorter in others. It has a great look and especially when there is snow settling on it. It adds a lot of mass and feels powerful, so some of my early creatures had suggestions of that in their hides. One of the other things I played around with was putting a blubbery seal or walrus hide on some of my concepts, something which I don't recall seeing before in a film creature. It was quite gross, which wasn't a bad association to have, considering we were designing mounts for the bad guys to ride.

Paul Tobin, Weta Workshop Designer

LCC
WW

AJB
WW

PT
WW

PT
WW

NK
WW

In thinking about potential riding beasts for the Orcs I tried to imagine creatures that might move in ways that were distinct from the Wargs or horses. I was also keen to avoid inventing a completely new monster.

Looking at all the creatures of Middle-earth that Tolkien invented, there are certain unwritten laws that unite them. They are hard to define, but it seems obvious to me when a creature defies them. There are no chimaeras in Middle-earth, creatures that combine the anatomy of different species the way many of the exotic beings in Greek mythology do,

for example, but there are creatures that borrow traits and assume them, like the vampires and were-beings of the First Age. Something Tolkien did do, however, was take real-world animals and give them a Middle-earth spin, like his Wargs and the Oliphaunts, so I felt more comfortable extrapolating new creatures based on slightly reimagined Earthly species than imposing completely novel beasts on Tolkien's world.

That thinking led me to the notion of a war ape. I liked the idea of a kind of huge, aggressive, boreal ape that could move very quickly, scaling cliff-faces or the walls of Dale. Tolkien

obliquely referenced apes in Middle-earth by describing Orcs as looking like 'the apes of the South' so there was some justification. My twist was making these creatures apes of the North, adapted to mountainous, cold climates. I figured Bergmann's Rule applied in Middle-earth too, which meant they could, and should, be big!

Daniel Falconer, Weta Workshop Designer

The Orcs' war beasts represented design at its purest for us, but possibly also most challenging, because we were trying to come up with new archetypes, original creatures that would surprise and excite, but that nonetheless sat comfortably within the established bestiary of Middle-earth. Our designers cast their creative net very wide, with creatures as diverse as primates, giant worms, serpents, moles and weasel-like monsters, as well as things that defied classification or straddled species in some disturbing way.

Richard Taylor,
Weta Workshop Design & Special Effects Supervisor

I offered up some little ferret-like beasties for the Orcs to take into battle (*top right*). It was in response to the need for something fast-moving and slinky that could dodge and weave through tight spaces, like the sewers or tunnels under Dale. When those scenes changed they became redundant, but for a while Peter was quite keen on them.

Andrew Baker, Weta Workshop Designer

Everyone was playing around with very bulky riding creatures so I thought I would try going the other way and offer some ideas that were spindly, with a little squad of Goblins climbing up and strapping themselves on its back. Peter quite liked it, I think because it was different.

Paul Tobin, Weta Workshop Designer

There was a brief from Peter to come up with a way to move the Orc army to the Lonely Mountain undetected. One of the ideas we were asked to explore was burrowing creatures that might dig tunnels into the ground through which the Orcs could travel; so we looked at different kinds of creatures, from big to small. Some of them were mammalian while others were like giant worms.

Andrew Baker, Weta Workshop Designer

I imagined Sauron was dredging the bottom of the pool for his fighting creatures, so we might see some very messed up, corrupt-looking things show up with the Orc army. Maybe some of these were the sorts of things he was breeding in the depths of Dol Guldur? We had mole-like things and rodent creatures, worm-like things, a plethora of nasty stuff. I always liked to tie the ideas back to things that Tolkien either hinted at or obliquely suggested in his writings. The term were-wyrm was thrown around. I think Peter was perhaps imagining something literally worm-like, but to me wyrm means something draconic, so I offered suggestions that had serpentine qualities and might have been distantly related to Dragons, without treading on Smaug's territory. I think one of the creatures I find particularly fascinating in our own world is the leopard seal, so one of the riding creatures I proposed was a kind of terrestrial leopard seal-like predator that I imagined might have been brought down from the ice wastes and bred as a war mount.

Greg Tozer, Weta Workshop Designer

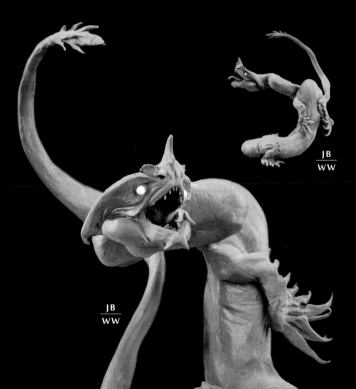

WARGS OF WAR

The armour of the Wargs is as much to attack as defend. There are historical instances of canine armour (though it is not sure it ever reached a battlefield), but for the Wargs the forward-pointing metal prongs and teeth of their *chanfreins* and *poitrails* enabled them to magnify the already formidable power of their fangs.

John Howe, Concept Art Director

WAR TROLLS & OGRES

I've always had a fond spot for Trolls, probably because the Cave-troll of Balin's Tomb was the first creature we designed and then sculpted as a large scannable maquette for *The Lord of the Rings*. While not explicitly mentioned in the text of the book as being present at the Battle of the Five Armies, Peter was keen to see a variety of Trolls brought to the fight. As we saw in the Battle of the Pelennor Fields, Trolls seem to be a natural extension of an Orc army, like the Middle-earth equivalent of a tank division, so it made sense they would be in attendance, either by choice or dragged along as heavy weapons under Orc control.

Richard Taylor,
Weta Workshop Design & Special Effects Supervisor

Thinking about a new kind of Troll for the battle sequences, I thought of putting great big scythe-like shields on the creature's long arms. Having shields that doubled as weapons was something we had done with the Orc soldiers. The Trolls were dragged along with the Orcs so it made sense that they would have things in common, so the shields I put on my Troll concept were reminiscent of the Orc army shields but with exaggerated blades. It was also a conscious homage to the armoured Trolls from *The Return of the King*.

Nick Keller, Weta Workshop Designer

GH
WW

NK
WW

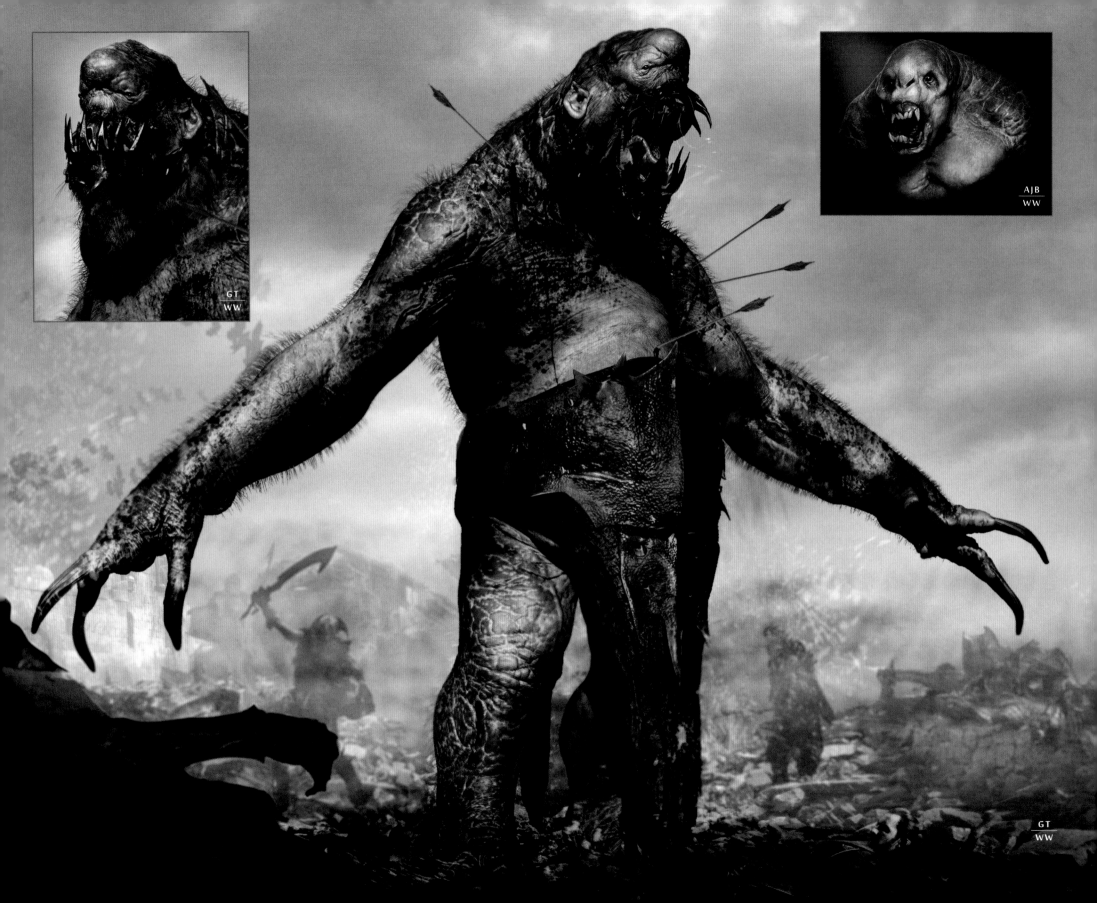

eter wanted to see all sorts of Trolls, so some of those I offered up were a little slimmer, with horny protrusions on their hide that are more like scales, something that Tolkien actually mentioned. I wanted to suggest something quite demonic and malicious. I was thinking of the Olog-hai from the books.

We came up with designs for a very specific Troll that eter asked for who would play a role in Alfrid's demise. he concept was that Alfrid was looking for somewhere to ide and inadvertently ended up being catapulted across the attlefield to finish in the monster's mouth. The Troll I offered eter was born without particularly impressive dentition, o instead he had some nasty-looking metal enhancements one, like a giant bear trap riveted to his face. I can't imagine hat does much to help his disposition, and that's a horrible mouth to accidentally end up in.

Greg Tozer, Weta Workshop Designer

Dan Hennah said to me one day, 'You have a day to go ave some fun in the battle.' Dan had done a napkin sketch f a Troll with a huge catapult on its back. I had a go at vorking that up into a drawing with this crazy Goblin-esque ontraption precariously rigged on and a steering nose ring hat a couple of characters would tug on. Another idea I ketched quickly was a Troll that had boarding ladders and climbing apparatus with a mechanism that I worked out o that he could convey soldiers right up onto the parapets f the city.

Anthony Allan, Concept Artist

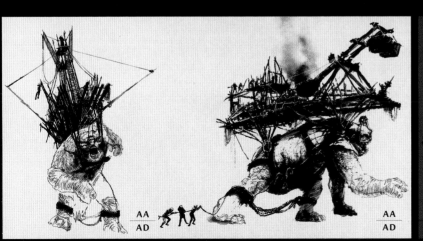

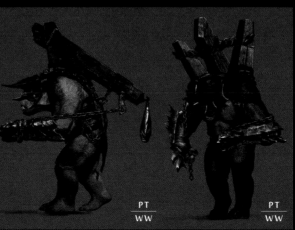

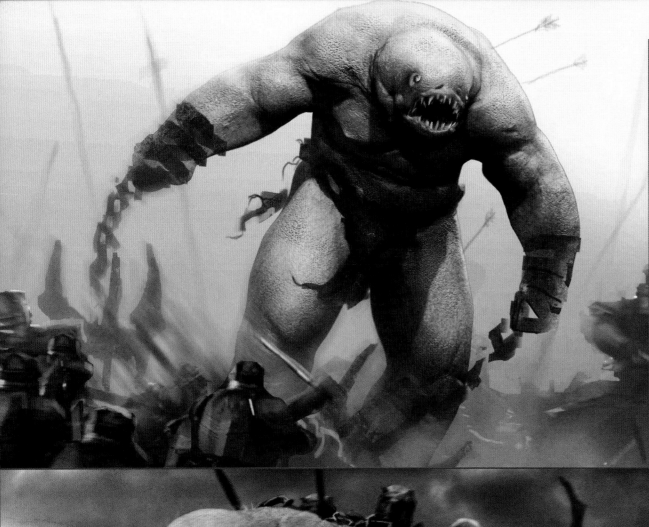

There was one Troll that we called the Bofur Troll because he was designed around a scene in which Bofur and his buddies would hijack a Troll being ridden by Orcs and steer him back into Azog's army. Peter had something quite specific in mind. He wanted a kind of big baby-faced creature that would seem quite stupid on the battlefield, not sure what it was doing and having to be led by its handlers. The audience might even feel sorry for it. It had sutured eyes and stubs for limbs onto which the Orcs had strapped flails.

We were looking for thrown weapons that we could put a unique spin on. I came up with the idea of these Trolls that could potentially walk up to the top of a ridge and hurl giant cabers, essentially giant, spiked tree-trunks, to go crashing down the mountainside, wiping out armies of guys. Peter suggested adding lots of chains with hammerheads and blades coming off them so these would all fly around as the caber careened down the hill, making it an even more terrifying-looking weapon. Rather than be a kind we had seen before, I tried to make the Troll himself something a little different too, a new variety.

Andrew Baker, Weta Workshop Designer

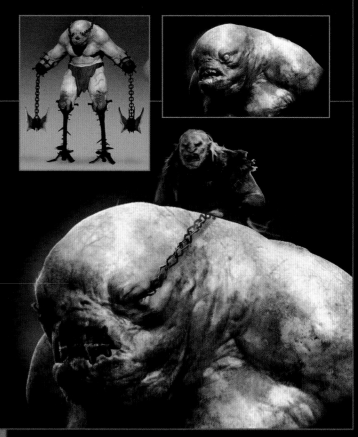

During Bilbo's riddle game with Gollum in the book of *The Hobbit*, there is a passing reference to an Ogre. It is the only time such a creature is mentioned in Tolkien's writings, but it afforded us a tantalizing opportunity to assign a name legitimately derived from the source material to a new class of being that might sit somewhere between the largest Orcs and the smaller Trolls.

Daniel Falconer, Weta Workshop Designer

Our brief was to conceive some battle creatures that weren't Orcs or Trolls but maybe sat somewhere in between. I imagined this particular character (*below*) as slow and sluggish, waving around a fairly simple spiked club and wearing little armour. This guy wouldn't be high on the intelligence scale and I imagined that his weapons and gear were probably given to him by whomever he served. I tried to keep the features and physiology simian-derived and not too complicated or fanciful.

Andrew Baker, Weta Workshop Designer

AJB
WW

BATS

Bats are such unusual and sometimes freakish-looking creatures that we didn't have to go far from what's already in nature to come up with something cool for the bat swarm that showed up at the Battle of the Five Armies. The horseshoe bat is a real animal, but it looks like it's straight out of a movie.

Greg Tozer, Weta Workshop Designer

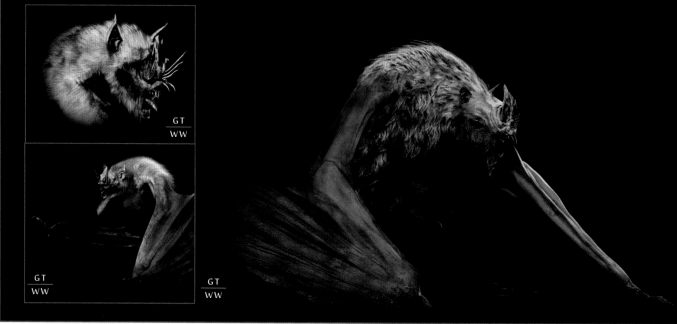

When Peter decided that Legolas was going to fly by bat to Ravenhill, that set the size of the bats at something just capable of supporting a character as large as an Elf, but not so large that it could fly off with him without difficulty. With a good idea of how big they needed to be, I tried to imagine what kind of creature the bats would be. They really just needed to be repulsive, nasty-looking things, perhaps mangy and unwell looking. I thought that, given that bats don't rely on their eyes to navigate in darkness, perhaps they would be deliberately blinded, with their eyes stitched over by their Orc wranglers. Presumably it makes them easier to manage or train, because they are definitely part of the Orc army and not just along for the scraps.

Alan Lee, Concept Art Director

I had painted a picture of Legolas grabbing hold of a bat to escape a situation he was in. Peter liked it but wanted to take it further, with Legolas hanging upside down and shooting arrows down into the Orcs.

Gus Hunter, Weta Workshop Designer

Goblin Armour & Weapons

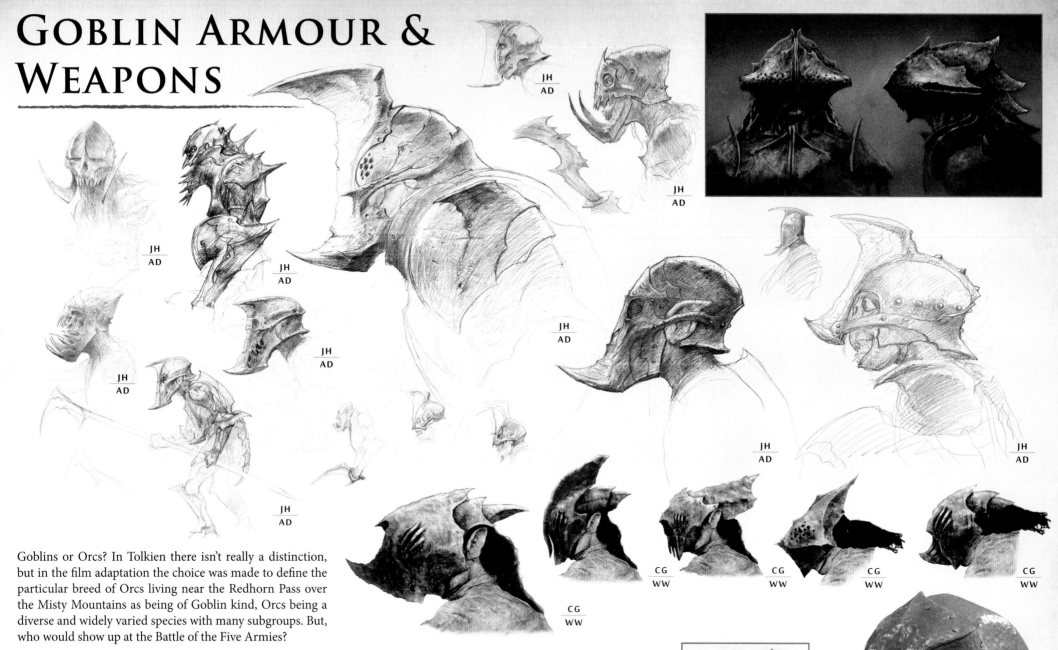

JH / AD
JH / AD
JH / AD
JH / AD
JH / AD
JH / AD
JH / AD
JH / AD
JH / AD
JH / AD
CG / WW
CG / WW
CG / WW
CG / WW
CG / WW
CG / WW
SL / WW
LCC / WW

Goblins or Orcs? In Tolkien there isn't really a distinction, but in the film adaptation the choice was made to define the particular breed of Orcs living near the Redhorn Pass over the Misty Mountains as being of Goblin kind, Orcs being a diverse and widely varied species with many subgroups. But, who would show up at the Battle of the Five Armies?

For a long time the army was to be the late Goblin King's forces, now presumably commanded by Azog, and was essentially an army of scrappy Goblins. A significant amount of design work went into the Goblin armour and weapons so when the change was made to an army of almost exclusively larger Orcs, some of the bold shape language explored for Goblin helmets and weapons was adapted and helped inform the Orc armour that was developed.

Daniel Falconer, Weta Workshop Designer

The army from Gundabad is complemented by Orcs from other Orcish strongholds. As the scripts developed, the importance of Bolg and the Gundabad Orcs became clear; it was Bolg and Azog who would lead the Orc army from the north. However, it is possible a few of the braver Goblins would have joined them, possibly travelling north in the shadow of the Misty Mountains and joining the armies marching south from Gundabad

John Howe, Concept Art Director

We pursued a very specific look for the Goblins for a while that was quite interesting. The idea was that they would avoid sunlight at all costs, so perhaps their armour was constructed in such a way that it provided shade for them as they moved about outside their caves. There was something like a carapace over them that doubled as a shield and protector against sunlight, but they would still be quite dextrous. They'd look like a swarm of beetles crawling over the landscape, and up and down walls or scaling mountainsides, in a way that was very nonhuman.

Andrew Baker, Weta Workshop Designer

AJB
WW

AJB
WW

AL
AD

TAKING RAVENHILL

BATTLE AMID THE DWARVEN RUINS

The Dwarven watchtower complex of Ravenhill perched atop a steep-sided spur of rock, overlooking the city of Dale. Like Dale, it was a deserted ruin by the time Thorin and his Company reclaimed the Mountain from the Dragon Smaug, but would become the location of a key set-piece in the Battle of the Five Armies. The fortress's strategic position made it sought-after real estate during the battle, with Azog claiming it as his headquarters. Thorin would lead a desperate sortie down the valley and up the precipitous slopes on the Mountain to attack the fortress in a bid to decapitate the enemy army by removing its leadership. With Fili, Kili and Dwalin at their king's side, and Legolas and Tauriel following them into the fray, the final confrontation between Thorin and Azog, flanked by his most fearsome warriors and grotesque son Bolg, takes place amid the crumbling ruins.

Ravenhill's design began as a simple tower but the importance and complexity of the action that would take place there saw the complex grow into a much larger structure with ancillary buildings, an ice lake and frozen waterfall. Its design spanned years, with the final shape of the fortress remaining undefined until the very end, when the pivotal drama it would stage was pinned down and mapped.

THE BATTLE IN THE VALLEY

Azog claims Ravenhill, with its commanding view of the valley below, as his headquarters. Peter also tried to conceptualize the spectacle and character of the battle itself from a distance, calling on Gus Hunter's exceptional ability to visualize large-scale environments and scenes. Joined by Eduardo Pena, Gus worked up sweeping vistas of atmospheric battle imagery.

It speaks to Peter's collegiate quality that as his thinking focussed on the details of the Battle of the Five Armies he assembled a think-tank from across the departments and companies and invited ideas. An outpouring of creativity followed. Team members at the Previs Department offered animatics, John Howe and Alan Lee drew furiously, Stunt Co-ordinator Glenn Boswell threw ideas in, and our design team at Weta Workshop generated storyboard sequences and production illustrations featuring all kinds of battle mayhem.

Richard Taylor,
Weta Workshop Design & Special Effects Supervisor

We had rampaging giant Trolls, ice lake skirmishes, chariot chases and heart-rending moments of sacrifice and loss. We were trying to think of moments for all our characters during the Battle of the Five Armies in which they might have a chance to do something heroic or climactic. With Thorin leading a group to confront Azog at Ravenhill I thought perhaps there was a chance for Balin to step up and take command of the Dwarves and Elves left behind in the valley. Maybe Balin was wounded, but the other Dwarves hoist him onto a shield to stand above the army and lead the counter-offensive?

Paul Tobin, Weta Workshop Designer

Alan Lee is a master. Something I learned from him was that it is very boring to stage a battle on flat, even ground. It makes a piece of artwork and a scene so much more interesting when the ground is broken or slopes away. Alan is so good at creating natural topography and I always tried to bear that in mind in my own work (*below, left & middle*).

Anthony Allan, Concept Artist

EP
WW

We had many brainstorming sessions with Peter and basically let loose with crazy ideas and gags, gags, gags! He wanted a grab bag of situations from which he could pull things out to create sequences.

We wanted to use situations in the course of the battle to show the Dwarves fighting as a team, jumping off each other's shoulders and that sort of thing.

Bombur picks up a kind of brazier, an Orc weapon on a huge chain. Bombur being Bombur, he completely steals the limelight and swings this weapon around, taking everything out in a circle around him. In another part of the battle Bofur and his buddies would hijack a blind Troll and steer him into his allies, pummelling them.

Gus Hunter, Weta Workshop Designer

RAVENHILL

AL
AD

AL
AD

Ravenhill fortress is a lookout post positioned on a rocky outcrop between the Dwarf realm of Erebor and the City of Dale. It overlooks the road to the Lonely Mountain and its Front Gate and was used as an early warning outpost for any would-be attack on the rich mines of Erebor. It was built by the Dwarves in their particular architectural style and recalls the aesthetics of the Mountain's interior. Giant slabs of green marble were mined to construct the watchtower fortress.

The approach to Ravenhill is via a bridge that spans the waterfall that pours from the tarn beside the fortress. It has been uninhabited since Smaug's attack and possession of Erebor.

Given Ravenhill's commanding position it holds great strategic value, with the potential to decide the outcome of the Battle of the Five Armies in the hands of whoever holds the hill. The Orc attack takes place in mid-winter and their forces are able to attack Ravenhill's defenders across the frozen tarn. This same body of ice will also see Thorin Oakenshield, King under the Mountain, and his arch nemesis Azog the Defiler meet for their final, fateful confrontation.

Dan Hennah, Production Designer

JH
AD

JH
AD

For a scene that would later be dropped, we imagined a bronze statuary group that the intense blast of Smaug's flame would have melted and bent decades earlier. It was designed to provide evidence of the fierce heat of Smaug's Dragon-fire. The statues also gave the audience an instantly recognizable feature that Gandalf would see in a vision of Bilbo in mortal danger. The Wizard would later recognize the same statue in the nick of time to save him, during the heat of battle.

John Howe, Concept Art Director

Ravenhill went through many versions, though it did retain throughout the slanting shards of rock overhanging the Long Valley above Dale. The outcrop has not only been tunnelled into (Peter imagined very early on that it was built by the Dwarves, though I believe Tolkien doesn't tell us who the builders were) but augmented by the solid masonry of the Dwarves. The raven motifs appeared early in the design process as well and were carried throughout.

John Howe, Concept Art Director

JH
WD

JH
WD

JH
WD

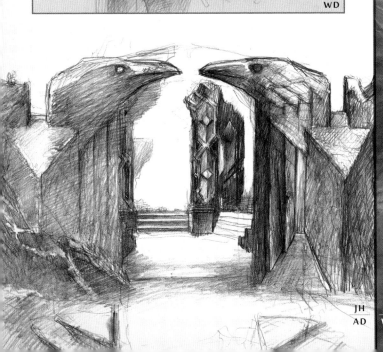

JH
AD

JH
WD

JH
WD

Ravenhill grew over the years. The first designs were little more than a few rocks and the remains of a fortified lookout post with a crumbling wall and tower, very much as Tolkien described. As the action that was to take place up there developed, it accumulated other aspects and kept growing into more of a small fortress built on a spur of rock.

We never defined whether Ravenhill was already ruined prior to Smaug's arrival or whether it was another casualty of his destructive entrance, like Dale, but I tend to prefer imagining that he gave it a swipe either during the first attack or later. We did quite a lot of damage to the structure in our designs, trying to create something that would be spooky and skeletal, especially when seen through the mist of low cloud clinging to the mountainside. Because that was how it would be seen the design task was to create depth and interesting and eerie silhouettes that would play against each other as the camera and cloud passed by it.

We needed the main structure to be tall and have visibility because Peter decided that Azog would kill one of the Dwarves there and that the others would see his body fall. It had several levels and would be a sort of trap. We built two sets as part of the complex but also shot them to double for other parts of the ruin; so the trick for us was to take those elements that were shot and reproduce them in different parts of the overall structure, building a cohesive environment that would be knitted together with digital extensions and wideshots.

The idea of the ice river or lake was an element that I had in one of my landscape photographs from our location tour and had incorporated into my artwork for the environment of the battle in the valley. I thought it would offer an interesting terrain feature to perhaps choreograph part of the action, with a slippery surface and the option for characters to fall through the ice. I was inspired by Sergei Eisenstein's film *Alexander Nevsky* in which the battle on the ice provides a very dramatic climax. Peter liked the ice element and it dovetailed nicely with his desire to see Ravenhill become much more of a focus for the decisive action of the battle, so we ended up putting a frozen river next to the main body of the fortress. It divided the structure and gave us a dramatic place to stage action like Thorin's fight, with the frozen waterfall perilously close.

A second, narrow, broken tower was added on the far side of the fall, based on an idea originally pitched by Weta Workshop's designers for Dale during our thinktank meetings.

Alan Lee, Concept Art Director

AL
WD

AL
WD

AL
WD

JH
WD

JH
WD

THE BATTLE AT RAVENHILL

We pitched all kinds of different ways for the confrontation at Ravenhill to unfold. There were a lot of characters' fates to wrap up and plot in terms of order and position. We knew which characters were going to be present and who needed to be near whom for the resolution that Peter, Fran and Philippa were writing, but the filmmakers had invited us to offer ideas in a series of thinktank meetings including the Previs team, Weta Workshop core design crew, and John Howe and Alan Lee. It was a great opportunity that we all embraced.

Paul Tobin, Weta Workshop Designer

AL
WD

GH
WW

GH
WW

GT
WW

MP
WD

From a story point of view, the most important battle arena in the entire Five Armies conflict was what was going on up at Ravenhill, where Thorin, Fili, Kili, Dwalin, Azog and Bolg would all end up, as well as Bilbo, Legolas and Tauriel. As a group we sat down and tried to rationalize how the action might progress, plotting intertwining pathways for our characters through the location and offering ideas for how their confrontations might unfold. Ultimately Peter chose what he liked and worked it into his screenplay.

Greg Tozer, Weta Workshop Designer

Peter settled on the idea of Thorin and Dwalin leading a desperate charge up from the field of battle to Ravenhill intending to kill Azog, who was leading his troops from the fortress with signals. Their path would take them down the ice river on a careening war chariot, encountering Wargs and Trolls, and then up the slope mounted on rams cut free from the chariot. There they would engage Orc troops occupying the ruins. Dwalin and Thorin would battle Orc mercenaries while Fili and Kili entered the eerily silent fortress and become separated.

Alan Lee, Concept Art Director

By this time Bilbo has arrived at Ravenhill with word of the massive army that is about to overwhelm them. Bolg was coming with his force of Orc warriors from Gundabad.

Alan Lee, Concept Art Director

One of the pair-ups on our checklist to bring together somewhere in the battle was Kili and Tauriel, because these characters' stories were on a trajectory together that we knew was leading to Kili's death. It made sense that Tauriel would do something desperate to try to prevent this, or that Kili would somehow give his life for hers. In one concept I pitched, Tauriel would take an incredible leap across a chasm to try to reach him in time.

Paul Tobin, Weta Workshop Designer

In the course of the battle Fili would find himself separated and alone inside the Ravenhill ruin, where Azog and his bodyguards capture him. Within sight of Thorin and Kili, who are both too far away to help, the young Dwarf is killed by the pale Orc, who discards Fili's body over the edge of the broken balcony.

Alan Lee, Concept Art Director

Legolas and Tauriel arrive at Ravenhill to help. Tauriel is seeking out Kili, who is looking to avenge his brother, but instead finds Bolg, with whom she fights. Kili rushes to help her but is slain. Tauriel grabs Bolg and takes him with her over the edge of the precipice, plunging down to land broken partway down the rocky cliff face.

Alan Lee, Concept Art Director

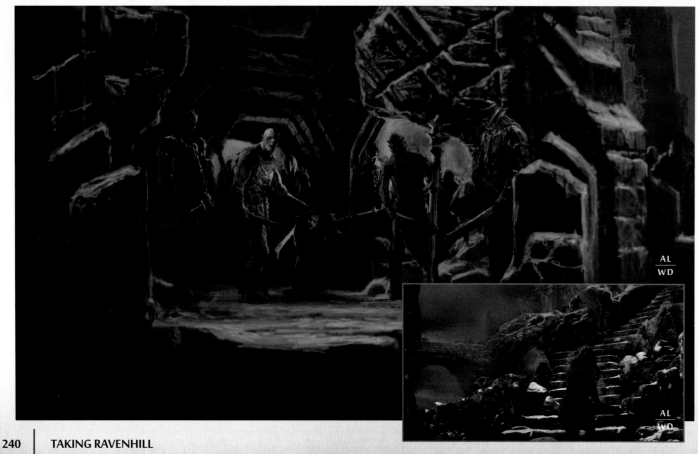

Legolas had to run out of arrows at least once in these movies and the perfect opportunity arose to have that happen when we were looking for a reason to have him engage Bolg mano-a-mano. Lacking an arrow to notch, he innovates and builds himself a bridge to close the gap between him and Bolg, who has survived his fall in better shape than Tauriel and now threatens her.

Daniel Falconer, Weta Workshop Designer

Up a tower on the far side of the ice waterfall from Tauriel and Bolg, Legolas must get across the gap. He casts his useless bow aside and leaps from the structure onto a Troll, jamming his sword, Orcrist, into the Troll's brain. The Troll careens into the tower and knocks it over, spanning the gap so that

Legolas can join Bolg in battle on the crumbling masonry to finish the fight they began in Lake-town in the previous film.

Alan Lee, Concept Art Director

The idea was suggested that Bolg and Legolas would battle in a collapsing tower. Peter really liked the potential for the very cool action sequence that gave him. We offered up different ideas for moments in the battle, like Legolas using his blades to slow him down in a fall, cutting into the timber beams. Bolg would hurl huge chunks of stone at Legolas, weakening the structure further until eventually it falls apart completely and Bolg is killed.

Gus Hunter, Weta Workshop Designer

Azog and Thorin had to have an epic showdown. I thought perhaps they could battle across the face of a frozen waterfall with huge chunks of ice falling away as they fought.

Gus Hunter, Weta Workshop Designer

Peter responded with enthusiasm to the idea of the frozen waterfall. There were some very cinematic things that could be done with the ice. A very strong visual that came out of our brainstorming sessions with Peter and the Previs team was the notion of the falls turning the colour of blood.

Peter was keen to see an ice lake at Ravenhill. In the course of discussion it seemed like this was going to be where Azog and Thorin would finally face off. I loved the idea of these two characters slugging it out, sodden and weary in slushy, ice-choked shallows. I imagined Azog being armoured in black to contrast his skin, with a cloak of black bear-skin that would beef-up his shoulders even more and create this huge silhouette, looming over Thorin. Not knowing at the time where Fili and Kili would meet their ends in the sequence, I worked up a very fast colour sketch of Azog holding Kili underwater while Thorin struggled desperately through the ice to reach him.

Daniel Falconer, Weta Workshop Designer

One of the things we had to accomplish in the course of the battle was returning Orcrist to Thorin. Thranduil had confiscated the Elven sword when he captured the Dwarves in Mirkwood; subsequent to that Legolas had taken it with him when he went in search of Tauriel, which meant we had a way of getting it to the scene of the battle. My idea was that Legolas would witness Thorin in his climactic fight with Azog. He was backed up near the edge of the frozen waterfall at Ravenhill and Legolas was below, on some crumbling masonry where he would confront Bolg. The Dwarf was outflanked and about to be dispatched when Legolas hurled the sword, impaling the Orc that was about to backstab Thorin. Thorin would wheel around and grip the hilt of Orcrist, pulling it clear as the Orc fell away over the side and bringing it round to block Azog's would-be killing blow, giving them a moment eye to eye before they launched into their final melee.

Paul Tobin, Weta Workshop Designer

Tauriel is saved, Bolg is gone, but Kili and Fili are dead. Legolas has thrown Thorin his sword and now the Dwarf and Azog are locked in battle at the edge of the frozen falls. The fight ends with Thorin killing the Orc who slew his grandfather and nephew, but he is also fatally wounded.

When all seems lost the Great Eagles arrive and with them, Beorn, who carves his way through the Orcs and bears Thorin out. The tide is turned and the battle is won for our heroes, but at a terrible cost.

Alan Lee, Concept Art Director

BEORN

Beorn steps into *The Hobbit* straight from Norse legend and myth, taking on, in Bilbo's naïve view, the form of a tall burly vegetarian beekeeper with a gruff demeanour. Beyond that, though, Beorn is something much grimmer. He is the last of the Beornings, and very much the Nordic skin-changer, the berserker able to change at will into a gigantic bear. He is the perfect inhabitant of Wilderland, neither friend nor foe, at least when Gandalf initially introduces his unexpected guests (and, like the Ents, he has no particular fondness for Dwarves).

John Howe, Concept Art Director

We were brainstorming ideas for key moments in the battle and I had an idea for Beorn's arrival. We had been told that the Great Eagles were going to be bringing Beorn with them when they showed up to turn the tide of the battle. My notion was that when he got airdropped in he would land on the surface of the frozen lake that Peter wanted up at Ravenhill. I thought it would make for a spectacular and dramatic entrance as he smashes through the ice, scattering the enemy. I have seen film of bears coming out of rivers when catching salmon and they can look very cool as they emerge, shaking water from their fur. He would transform as he fell, changing from man to bear and then burst out, carving his way through enemies to get to where Thorin and Azog were. In the book he bore a near-dead Thorin out of the battle so I was picturing something like that moment and trying to stage it dramatically (*storyboard sequence, left*).

Paul Tobin, Weta Workshop Designer

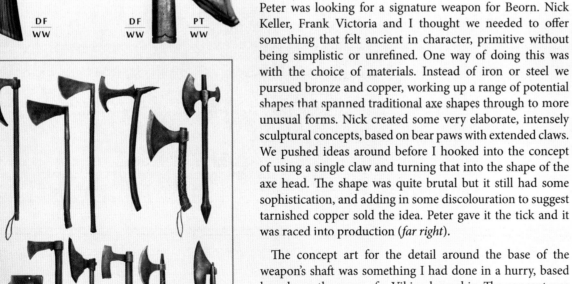

Beorn's axes were intended to reflect the mythic, wild aspects of his character, but in the end the only axe we would see in the films was a simple woodcutter's axe in his home. Beorn's weapons are his fangs and talons.

John Howe, Concept Art Director

Peter was looking for a signature weapon for Beorn. Nick Keller, Frank Victoria and I thought we needed to offer something that felt ancient in character, primitive without being simplistic or unrefined. One way of doing this was with the choice of materials. Instead of iron or steel we pursued bronze and copper, working up a range of potential shapes that spanned traditional axe shapes through to more unusual forms. Nick created some very elaborate, intensely sculptural concepts, based on bear paws with extended claws. We pushed ideas around before I hooked into the concept of using a single claw and turning that into the shape of the axe head. The shape was quite brutal but it still had some sophistication, and adding in some discolouration to suggest tarnished copper sold the idea. Peter gave it the tick and it was raced into production (*far right*).

The concept art for the detail around the base of the weapon's shaft was something I had done in a hurry, based loosely on the prow of a Viking long ship. The concept was that it would depict Beorn on all fours and then turning and rearing up. I was on my way out of the country and didn't get to finish it so poor old Nick had to clean up my hasty sketch and turn it into the beautiful piece of carved pattern work that ended up on the finished prop.

Paul Tobin, Weta Workshop Designer

THERE &
BACK AGAIN

A HOBBIT GOES HOME

War weary and wiser, Bilbo says his goodbyes to friends fallen and found in Erebor and Dale before taking his leave of the world of Dwarves, Dragons and battles to look west once again. Accompanied by Gandalf, the hobbit retraces his steps in lighter company and weighed down only by his pack. Passing through the Trollshaw Forest, he collects the two chests of treasure buried in the Trolls' den, which the Dwarves insisted he claim. By no means equal to the promised one-fourteenth share of the Treasure of Erebor, his souvenirs would nonetheless be counted a small fortune in Hobbiton. At the very least they would be a curiosity and source for speculation and gossip for generations to come.

Borne home by the promise of his armchair's embrace and a warm glow in his familiar hearth, Bilbo is surprised to find himself greeted by the spectacle of an auction in full swing outside his home. Lined up along Bagshot Row is an array of Bag End's contents, from silverware and crockery to wall hangings and furniture, being sold off in the wake of his apparent demise. It is only the producing of his contract with the Company of Thorin that assures the auctioneer of Bilbo's identity and puts an end to the bleeding of his property, much to the Sackville-Bagginses' disappointment.

Bilbo's return to the green hills of the Shire provided the perfect way to bookend the trilogy, dovetailing into *The Lord of the Rings* and offering counterpoint to the savagery and violence of the Battle of the Five Armies. The quaint predicament of Bilbo's property being auctioned contrasted with the world-threatening peril of Sauron's return and two armies of blood-lusting Orcs, reminding the audience of what was at stake and of the comforting isolation of the Shire, a true haven from the agendas and horrors of Wilderland.

Ironically, the scenes of Bilbo's return were among the first to be shot on location for the film trilogy. Although taking place a year later, in the story, Bilbo's return was shot at the same time as the early Hobbiton scenes from *An Unexpected Journey*, and long before any of the Lake-town or Erebor sequences were fully conceived or filmed.

BILBO

COSTUME & PROPS

We were asked to throw in some ideas for Bilbo's costume for his return journey to Hobbiton, wearing clothing from Lake-town, but it was surprisingly tough because at the time that part of the films hadn't been designed. We had no idea what the people of Lake-town would be dressed in. There were some very early costume sketches but no solid leads yet, so we were groping in the dark a bit. There had been some exploration around the idea of fish scales, so I ran with that for a tunic suggestion along with some Dwarven trophies like a shield and helmet. He was returning from his adventures with loot so I made him more princely, rather than bedraggled like you might be after such a long journey. I thought he should look exotic, rich and also just a tad dangerous, because he isn't the same hobbit he was when he left.

Paul Tobin, Weta Workshop Designer

Bilbo's costume for his return to Bag End maintained the blue cotton velvet costume he wore throughout his journey from Lake-town onwards, but we wrapped a rough-woven mauve silk cloak with a red hand-embroidered border around his shoulders, secured with a silver Dwarven clasp (*right*).

Ann Maskrey, Costume Designer

PT
WW

PT
WW

PT
WW

AM
CD

Bilbo's cloak was difficult to scale down for our small-scale double versions and I struggled to make a much-loved vintage embroidery stretch beyond the principal costume, but we got there in the end thanks to a lot of patchwork. I kept a tiny piece of the trim as a keepsake, hardly enough to cover a Lego figurine, but enough to remind me.

Ann Maskrey, Costume Designer

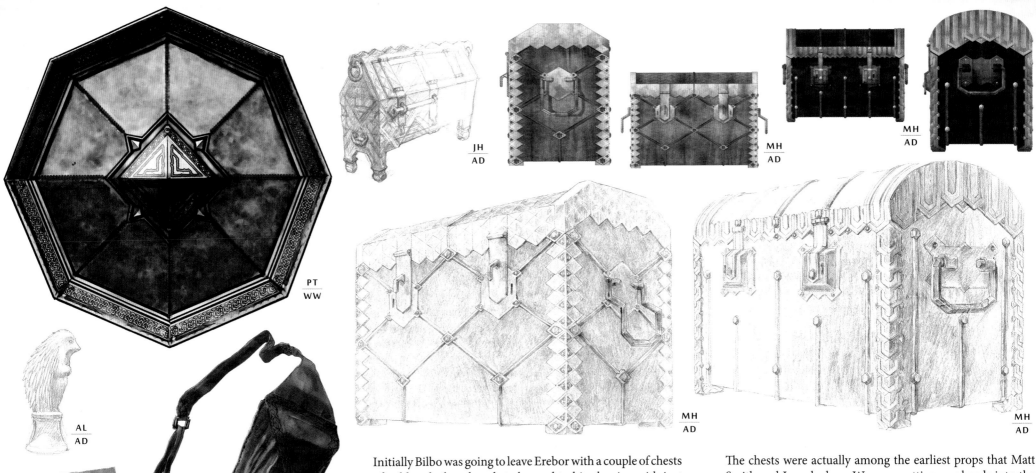

PT
WW

AL
AD

DR
AD

JH
AD

MH
AD

MH
AD

MH
AD

MH
AD

MH
AD

Coming so early, we didn't have any locked-down Dwarf shields yet, so Bilbo's Dwarf shield battle trophy was something that I pulled out of the air, referencing the Dwarven tendency toward angular geometry. In this case it was an octagonal rather than round shield. It was an unusual thing – a suggestion. I believe in the end the actual shield prop used might have ended up being a dusted-off piece of set dressing from Balin's Tomb in *The Lord of the Rings*.

Paul Tobin, Weta Workshop Designer

Initially Bilbo was going to leave Erebor with a couple of chests of gold and silver, but that changed to him leaving with just his pack and then later digging up and taking home the little stash of treasure that the Dwarves buried in the Trolls' cave during the first film. Later, when Frodo is looking through Bilbo's things in Bag End, we would see some specific items of treasure and mementos of his journey, including a claw, an Orc helmet, Sting, one of Beorn's carved chess pieces and the portrait that Ori had done of him, among other things.

Nick Weir, Prop Master

I think the gold and silver chests that Bilbo carried his treasure home in were some of the best props in the films. The gold chest, with a rounded top, was actually one that had already been made as a background piece but needed to be made prettier, so Mat Hunkin and I developed it. Based on how well it was reviewed we got to work up the silver one, with the flat top, from scratch.

Matt Smith, Prop Designer

The chests were actually among the earliest props that Matt Smith and I worked on. We were getting our heads into the Dwarven aesthetic and as we were working on them we were looking for reasons for those characteristic aesthetic details to exist. Everyone was putting angularity and hard geometry in the Dwarven work because it felt so natural for Dwarves, but the best design has a function or a philosophy that drives its form. We could put an angle anywhere, but where did it make sense to go? Why would the Dwarves have done it that way? Which angle would we choose? We were keen to make every choice justified and make sense. We thought about the chests being locked together with a certain structure with seven sides that reflected the seven Dwarf tribes, seven kings. There are shapes suggesting the Lonely Mountain. We had a paranoid eye in there, suggesting the eye of Smaug. The pencils were flying and our minds were going a million miles an hour. It was easy to get lost in Middle-earth! Sometimes we had to sit back and remind ourselves, 'It's just a movie, man! It's just a movie.' It was, but it was also a movie that we felt demanded that level of thought.

Mat Hunkin, Prop Designer

BAG END

AUCTION

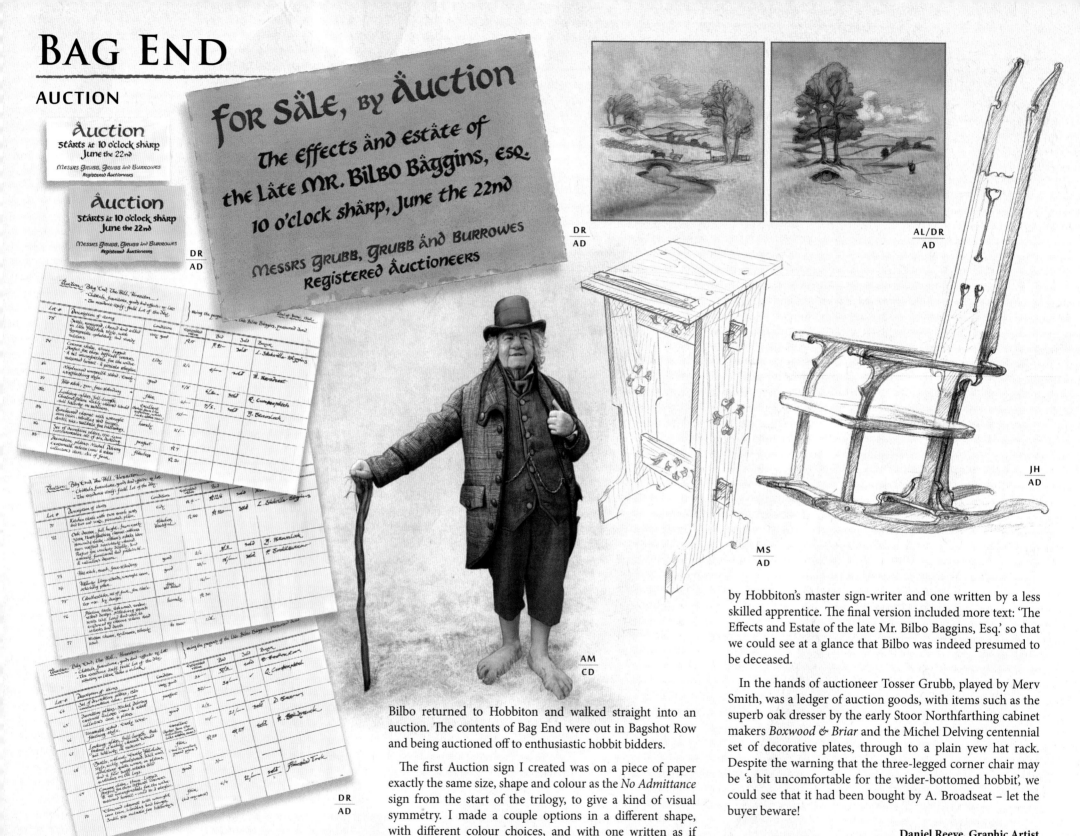

Bilbo returned to Hobbiton and walked straight into an auction. The contents of Bag End were out in Bagshot Row and being auctioned off to enthusiastic hobbit bidders.

The first Auction sign I created was on a piece of paper exactly the same size, shape and colour as the *No Admittance* sign from the start of the trilogy, to give a kind of visual symmetry. I made a couple options in a different shape, with different colour choices, and with one written as if by Hobbiton's master sign-writer and one written by a less skilled apprentice. The final version included more text: 'The Effects and Estate of the late Mr. Bilbo Baggins, Esq.' so that we could see at a glance that Bilbo was indeed presumed to be deceased.

In the hands of auctioneer Tosser Grubb, played by Merv Smith, was a ledger of auction goods, with items such as the superb oak dresser by the early Stoor Northfarthing cabinet makers *Boxwood & Briar* and the Michel Delving centennial set of decorative plates, through to a plain yew hat rack. Despite the warning that the three-legged corner chair may be 'a bit uncomfortable for the wider-bottomed hobbit', we could see that it had been bought by A. Broadseat – let the buyer beware!

Daniel Reeve, Graphic Artist

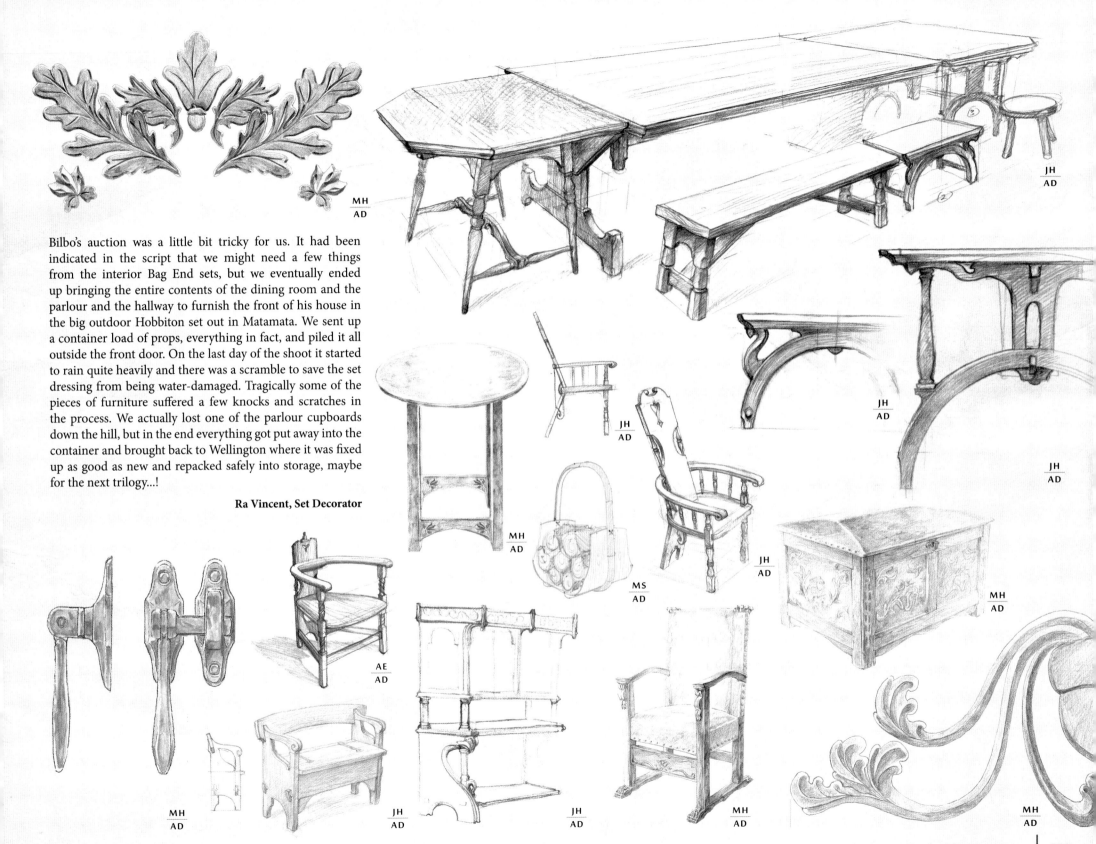

Bilbo's auction was a little bit tricky for us. It had been indicated in the script that we might need a few things from the interior Bag End sets, but we eventually ended up bringing the entire contents of the dining room and the parlour and the hallway to furnish the front of his house in the big outdoor Hobbiton set out in Matamata. We sent up a container load of props, everything in fact, and piled it all outside the front door. On the last day of the shoot it started to rain quite heavily and there was a scramble to save the set dressing from being water-damaged. Tragically some of the pieces of furniture suffered a few knocks and scratches in the process. We actually lost one of the parlour cupboards down the hill, but in the end everything got put away into the container and brought back to Wellington where it was fixed up as good as new and repacked safely into storage, maybe for the next trilogy...!

Ra Vincent, Set Decorator

THE BLACK ARROW

1:1 scale prop replica of Bard's Black Arrow prop as seen in the films, created at Weta Workshop based on designs by Concept Art Director John Howe. Measures more than two metres (almost seven feet) in length!

PORTRAIT OF BILBO BAGGINS™

1:1 scale accurate prop replica hand-aged by Graphic Artist Daniel Reeve, who created the prop for the films.

SMAUG™ MINIATURE STATUE

Miniature polystone statue by Weta Workshop Sculptors Greg Tozer and Gary Hunt.

STAFF OF SARUMAN THE WHITE

1:1 scale prop replica cast from the same moulds as the original prop designed for *The Lord of the Rings* by Concept Art Director Alan Lee and seen again in *The Hobbit: The Battle of the Five Armies*.

BARD THE BOWMAN

Limited edition 1/6th scale polystone statue by Weta Workshop Sculptor Gary Hunt.

RUNESTONE OF KILI™

Collectible replica of the prop designed by Alan Lee and created by the 3Foot7 Art Department.

The same burning passion and relentless pursuit of perfection that drives every department bringing Middle-earth to life for *The Hobbit: The Battle of the Five Armies* also goes into the creation of the most authentic movie replicas. Created by the same artists working on the films, Weta is sourcing beautiful Middle-earth artefacts from across the departments and companies represented in *The Hobbit: The Battle of the Five Armies*, and offering them as authentic replicas for discerning collectors.

The line represents the closest experience next to visiting Middle-earth itself. Collectors will find replica swords hand-forged by a world-renowned master swordsmith using centuries-old and cutting edge techniques and props cast from the very same moulds as those made for the films. Maps and calligraphic prop replicas have been handmade and the films' original artists have created new, limited edition art prints based on the characters and landscapes they helped imagine for the films.

CREDITS

Weta Workshop (WW)

Weta Workshop is a multi-award winning conceptual design and manufacturing facility based in Wellington, New Zealand. Best known for its Academy Award®-winning work on *The Lord of the Rings* trilogy, Weta Workshop has contributed conceptual design (creatures, characters and environments) for *The Hobbit* films along with manufacturing armour, weapons, specialty prosthetics and creatures. Weta Workshop is led by Academy Award® winner Richard Taylor.

Richard Taylor	Design & Special Effects Supervisor	
Andrew Baker	Weta Workshop Designer	AJB
Andrew Moyes	Weta Workshop Designer	AWM
Ben Mauro	Weta Workshop Designer	BM
Chris Guise	Weta Workshop Designer	CG
Daniel Falconer	Weta Workshop Designer	DF
David Meng	Weta Workshop Designer	DM
Ed Denton	Weta Workshop 3D Model Maker	ED
Eduardo Pena	Weta Workshop Designer	EP
Frank Victoria	Weta Workshop Designer	FV
Gary Hunt	Weta Workshop Sculptor	GJH
Greg Tozer	Weta Workshop Designer	GT
Gus Hunter	Weta Workshop Designer	GH
Jamie Beswarick	Weta Workshop Designer	JB
Lindsey Crummett	Weta Workshop Designer	LCC
Nick Keller	Weta Workshop Designer	NK
Paul Tobin	Weta Workshop Designer	PT
Steve Lambert	Weta Workshop Designer	SL
Steven Saunders	Weta Workshop Sculptor	SSA
Stuart Thomas	Weta Workshop Designer	ST

Weta Digital (WD)

Weta Digital is one of the world's premier visual effects companies. Led by Senior Visual Effects Supervisor Joe Letteri, Weta Digital is known for uncompromising creativity and commitment to developing innovative technology. Weta Digital established its reputation for cutting edge visual effects with work on blockbusters like *The Lord of the Rings* trilogy and *King Kong*. The company began work in 1993 on co-founder Peter Jackson's film *Heavenly Creatures* and is based in a number of facilities spread around Wellington, New Zealand. Weta Digital is creating all digital visual effects on *The Hobbit* films.

Gino Acevedo	Textures Supervisor/Creative Art Director	GA
Alan Lee	Concept Art Director	AL
John Howe	Concept Art Director	JH
Michael Pangrazio	Senior Art Director	MP

NB.   Film credits were not available at the time of publication.

ARTWORK CREDIT KEY

Artist credit as indicated on top and their department indicated beneath line	AL / AD
All artwork on page by indicated artist and department	AL / AD

ABOUT THE AUTHOR

Daniel Falconer has been a designer at Weta Workshop for more than seventeen years, producing conceptual art as part of the design team on many of the company's high profile projects including *The Lord of the Rings*, *King Kong*, *The Chronicles of Narnia*, *Avatar*, and now *The Hobbit*. In addition to the *Chronicles* series, Daniel has written a number of books for Weta; *The World of Kong*, *The Crafting of Narnia*, *Weta: The Collector's Guide* and *The Art of District 9*, each showcasing the company's creative works. He lives and works in Wellington, New Zealand with his wife Catherine and two daughters, revelling in his dream career of playing in imaginary worlds every day.